What's that
Snake?

What's that Snake?

A starter's guide to snakes of southern Africa

Johan Marais

A word from the author

Snakes are fascinating creatures that have been misunderstood and feared as a result of ignorance, superstition and myth. Recently, however, public interest in snakes has grown due to an increase in wildlife programmes and literature on the subject.

Snakes are fairly widespread in most regions, and you may wish to learn about the snakes in your area. If you regularly encounter snakes where you live, it is likely that there will be four or five common varieties.

Many species hunt actively for food, resulting in their occasional appearance in suburban gardens. There is no question that some of our snakes are potentially lethal because of their venom, but they are a minority. When faced with a dangerous species, never tamper with the snake or try to handle it. The majority of southern African snakes, however, are either harmless or possess mild venom. The symptoms from such a bite are less painful and threatening than those of a bee sting.

Snakes can be observed at national parks and game reserves. In arid regions you can spot them in trees, hunting for birds' eggs and hatchlings, and if you visit a waterhole you should keep an eye on communal weaver nests. Unfortunately, snakes are masters of disguise and are very quick to disappear, resulting in rather brief sightings. If you come across a snake, especially in a game reserve, try not to disturb it, and take lots of photographs. There is little doubt that such photographs will elicit more attention from your friends than most 'big five' photographs.

An ongoing Reptile Conservation Assessment, funded by the South African National Biodiversity Institute, accepts and collates digital photographs of snakes received from members of the public. These photographs are being used to confirm the presence of snakes in well-defined localities, and will be of value in future conservation programmes.

It can be quite difficult to identify southern African snakes, as coloration of species can vary significantly. This book deals with the more common groups of snakes – those you are most likely to encounter. The species are placed in 28 groups: some according to family; others according to common behaviour or appearance. The aim of this book is to help you identify group characteristics before identifying individual species. A field guide is a valuable companion to this text, and more detailed information on southern African snakes can be found in *A Complete Guide to the Snakes of Southern Africa* and *Field Guide to Snakes and other Reptiles of Southern Africa*.

Johan Marais

A Puff Adder moves through the sand, south of Windhoek, Namibia.

Cape Cobras may climb trees in the early evening to search for prey.

Acknowledgements

My lifelong passion for reptiles has taken me to wonderful places all over the world where I have met amazing people, some of whom have become very good friends. The snake fraternity has its characters, some rather strange but passionate; all of them interesting people. I have enjoyed my association with fellow herpetologists and have found them to be very helpful, hospitable and accommodating.

Time in the field is what most herpetologists live for and I have had many a good day scratching around with Paul Moler, Randy Babb, Gordon Setaro, Bill Branch, Aaron Bauer, Graham Alexander, Colin Tilbury and Donald Strydom. Through the years, several people have helped with advice, photographic sessions and have provided specimens to photograph. Although they are far too many to list, special thanks go to Bill Branch, Mike Bates, Don Broadley, Lynn Raw, Mike Jaensch, Barry Stander, Scotty Kyle, Mike Perry, Mike Griffin, Vincent Eagan and Rob Deans.

Several of the outstanding photographs in this book were supplied by friends – Warren Schmidt, Marius Burger, Graham Alexander, Tony Phelps, Bryan Maritz, Colin Tilbury, Randy Babb and Bill Branch.

I am grateful to my colleagues at Fascination Books, especially Alta Naude and my brother Nico Marais, for keenly filling the gaps during my extended absence. My daughter Melissa has always been a great inspiration and I thank her for all her love. My late father was always my greatest fan and supporter and I learnt a great deal from him.

Thanks to the Struik team – specifically Pippa Parker, Colette Alves, Robin Cox and Helen de Villiers – for their hard work, professionalism and dedication. My long association with Struik Publishers has been particularly pleasant and it has always been a pleasure to walk into their offices.

My very good friend Graham Alexander has always been there to answer my questions and has been very supportive. I thank my partner and soul mate Riaana for her patience, support, understanding and love. I look forward to many happy days in the field with her.

JOHAN MARAIS
2007

Struik Publishers
(a division of New Holland Publishing
(South Africa) (Pty) Ltd)
Cornelis Struik House
80 McKenzie Street
Cape Town 8001

New Holland Publishing is a division of Avusa Ltd

Visit us at **www.struik.co.za**
Log on to our photographic website **www.imagesofafrica.co.za**
for an African experience.

First published in 2007
2nd impression 2008

Copyright © published edition:
Struik Publishers, 2007
Copyright © text: Johan Marais, 2007
Copyright © photographs: Johan Marais, 2007 except where indicated

ISBN 978 1 77007 373 9

Publishing manager: **Pippa Parker**
Managing editor: **Helen de Villiers**
Editor: **Colette Alves**
Designer: **Robin Cox**
Proofreader: **Glynne Newlands**

Reproduction by Hirt & Carter Cape (Pty) Ltd
Printed and bound by Kyodo Printing Co (S'Pore) Pte Ltd

Front Cover (top): Southern Vine Snake
Front Cover (bottom): Coral Shield Cobra
Page 1: Aurora House Snake (Photo: Warren Schmidt)
Page 3: Boomslang (Photo: Warren Schmidt)

Contents

Introduction 10

Snake Groups
Large Adders **22**
Dwarf Adders **26**
Dune Adders **30**
Night Adders **32**
Mambas **34**
Non-spitting Cobras **36**
Spitting Snakes **40**
Coral Shield Cobras **44**
Shield Cobras **46**
Boomslang **48**
Vine Snakes **52**
Stiletto Snakes & Natal Black Snake **54**
Sand & Whip Snakes **56**
Skaapstekers **60**
Tiger Snakes **62**
Herald Snake **64**
Purple-glossed Snakes **66**
Pythons **68**
House & Rock Snakes **70**
Water Snakes **74**
Mole Snake **76**
Green Snakes **78**
Slug-eaters **80**
Wolf Snakes **82**
File Snakes **84**
Egg-eaters **86**
Blind Snakes **88**
Worm or Thread Snakes **90**

Glossary 92
Index of names 93

Introduction

Snakes have always had a bad reputation. Still today, newspapers and magazines give prominence to a snakebite, irrespective of the severity of the bite. Sadly, much of what is written about snakes in the press is inaccurate.

One hears rumours of snakes acting aggressively, and even chasing and attacking humans. More often than not, these reports are entirely unfounded. Snakes never chase after people: they do their utmost to avoid humans, and do not go out of their way to attack. Most snakes are retiring creatures and move away from such encounters as quickly as possible. Some snakes, such as the Puff Adder and Gaboon Adder, rely on camouflage to escape detection, and there is a danger of stepping on them, causing them to strike out in self-defence. But if you are a few metres away from any snake, it is improbable that it will advance and attack.

Myths and stories about snakes abound. There are myths about snakes that drink milk from cows, and that bite their own tails and roll down hills; deadly snakes that wait on branches and drop onto people walking beneath; and Puff Adder babies that eat their way out of their mother's uterus. Some people believe that snakes die only at sunset. It is also a popular fallacy that snakes move about in pairs, and that if you kill one you should burn it to prevent a revenge attack by its mate.

As most snakes are shy and secretive, encounters with them are quite uncommon and, even then, brief. Should you happen upon a snake, chances are that it will move off quickly and head

Despite its threatening appearance, the Rhombic Egg-eater has no teeth and is completely harmless.

The Gaboon Adder relies on its perfect camouflage to escape detection.

for the nearest hole or shrub. After recovering somewhat from the initial shock, the time you have to study it is very brief, and most people then tend to exaggerate the size of the snake when describing it.

Despite a growing awareness of the need for conservation, many people still needlessly kill snakes on sight. The majority of snakes in southern Africa are harmless, with only about 10% of species considered dangerous to humans. Some snakes play an important role in controlling pests, which is of direct benefit to humans. The Brown House Snake, for example, has the ability to enter a rodent burrow and eat an entire rodent family. Pythons are effective in controlling problem animals such as dassies and cane rats, which breed excessively and devour vegetation on farms.

How to behave if you encounter a snake

People encounter snakes from time to time in suburban gardens, on smallholdings and farms, in the wild, while hiking or fishing, or when visiting game reserves. Most of these snake/human encounters are brief. The snake is usually accidentally disturbed and darts off into the closest bush before it can be identified. Snakes that are active at night are not always that quick, and many of them will move off slowly. Others, like the Puff Adder, rely on camouflage and may remain motionless in one spot without attempting to escape.

Should you see a snake in your garden, do not try to kill it; in the majority of cases it will slip away harmlessly and not be seen again. If you are concerned about the snake, it is best to contact a snake enthusiast in your area and leave it to them to remove the snake. Tampering with snakes and trying to catch them can lead to trouble. If you do not know of a snake handler, you can seek assistance from the fire department, police, the local snake park or a natural history museum. It is important to remember that spitting snakes are able to eject their venom in excess of 2 m. It makes sense to exercise caution around snakes at all times.

In the wild there are only two recommended courses of action should you encounter a snake. If you are very close to the snake, stand perfectly still. Any snake, no matter how nervous or scared, will eventually calm down and try to escape, and will tend to ignore stationary objects. The snake may even slither over your feet, but it will move off without trying to bite, provided you stand very still. The second option, if you are a few metres away from the snake, is to walk away. It is not necessary to run, as snakes never chase people.

A Coral Shield Cobra in a defensive pose. Even when roused, this snake will not chase a person.

SNAKE HABITATS

Snakes are found in a wide variety of habitats throughout southern Africa. Many of the region's snakes have very specialized habitat requirements, while others are found over wide ranges and in diverse habitats. Because of suitable weather conditions, sufficient shelter and an abundance of food, coastal and low-lying areas, as well as parts of the arid west, tend to have far more snakes and greater diversity in snake species than higher altitude grasslands in the Highveld and Free State. However, a suitable habitat with ample food in a high-lying area could sustain large numbers of snakes.

As snakes occur in all habitat types, from coastal forest, fynbos, savanna and karoo to true desert, they may be encountered virtually anywhere in southern Africa.

FORESTS

Snakes such as the Green Mamba, Gaboon Adder and Forest Cobra frequent densely vegetated forests or their fringes. Other snakes with a far wider distribution, like the harmless green snakes, are also found in forest habitat. Forest snakes tend to live in dense vegetation, among the leaf litter on the forest floor, or in the ground – either down the burrows of other animals or in soft soil. Because of the abundance of vegetation, most forest snakes are difficult to see except when they bask in the sun.

The destruction of forests poses a threat to the survival of many creatures, including some snakes.

FYNBOS

The Mediterranean-type vegetation that is found from the Western Cape along the south coast to the Eastern Cape is commonly referred to as fynbos, and comprises a unique flora. Most of the snakes that occur in fynbos are also found in adjacent habitats, although some of the region's rarest snakes, such as the Southern Adder, are found only in fynbos. This habitat has suffered in recent years due to industrial and suburban development.

GRASSLAND

Several snakes have adapted to live in grassland, and some of the snakes found in this habitat are referred to as grass snakes. The Rinkhals also prefers grassland, where it inhabits rodent or other animal burrows.

The top of the KwaZulu-Natal Drakensberg is inhabited by snakes that favour the high altitude of mountainous areas, such as the Berg Adder.

Namaqualand is home to a great variety of snakes.

Rocky areas with narrow crevices are ideal for rock-living species such as the Spotted Rock Snake.

SAVANNA

Savanna may range from fairly arid areas that are sparsely grassed, with scattered trees, to areas with good rainfall that are wooded, sometimes densely so. A variety of snake species inhabit savanna regions, but most of them also occur in adjacent habitat.

KAROO

This vast area provides suitable habitat for a wide variety of snakes, ranging from some of the sand snakes that prefer open areas with sparse vegetation, to tiger snakes and Rhombic Egg-eaters, which are more at home in rocky areas. Other snakes that live in the karoo biome include Puff Adders, Cape Cobras, Brown House Snakes and Horned Adders. There are many microhabitats within this biome – such as rocky areas and sandy areas with karoo scrub – that provide suitable habitat for a variety of snakes. Few of the snakes in this habitat are active during the heat of the day, and good summer rain tends to coax snakes from their underground hideouts.

DESERTS

Few snakes have the ability to survive in desert conditions, although several species are found on the fringes of true desert. Péringuey's Adder and the Namaqua Dwarf Adder have adapted well to desert conditions. They worm themselves into soft sand to escape detection and the heat of the day. Their eyes are situated high up on the head, allowing them to see while buried in sand. They drink water off their bodies, which collects when mist clouds condense. These desert snakes sidewind, which enables them to negotiate soft sand and keeps most of the body off the hot surface. Several snakes leave distinctive tracks, especially when moving over soft sand.

Some species, such as dune adders, have adapted to living in desert conditions.

Finding snakes

Within each of the broader habitat zones, snakes seek out shelter in a number of places – under rocks, in bushes, in trees and even underground. Most snakes are ground-living, and are active exclusively either during the day or at night. They hide in rodent burrows, under rocks and logs, or in deserted termite mounds. In summer, diurnal snakes tend to be more active in the mornings, when they emerge from their hideouts and search for food or bask in the sun. Many of the nocturnal snakes become active at twilight and remain so until midnight, when their activity drops off dramatically.

There are many fossorial species – those that spend most of their lives underground. They are seldom encountered, except when they are exposed during digging or cleaning-up operations, or when forced to the surface after heavy rains. Tree-living snakes, such as the Boomslang, Green Mamba and some of the bush snakes, spend most of their lives in trees and shrubs, seldom venturing to the ground, where they are far more vulnerable. Some of these snakes have specially adapted scales on the belly with ridges or keels to assist climbing. Other species are rock-living, hiding in narrow crevices during the day and emerging in the early evening to look for food. The Spotted Rock Snake has a very flat body and head, making it particularly well adapted for hiding in rock crevices.

Should you wish to catch snakes, it is important to bear in mind that permits are required in most provinces, and that venomous snakes should never be handled by inexperienced people. You can find snakes by looking under stones and rocks. Take care not to damage the habitat, and rocks that are moved should be returned to their original position. Collectors place sheets of corrugated tin or asbestos in shaded areas, knowing that snakes will use them as refuges to hide beneath. In some areas, collectors gather specimens by driving along quiet tarred roads and catching snakes that cross the roads. This method of collecting is illegal in some provinces, and advice should be sought from the authorities prior to collecting. Snake enthusiasts often smash open deserted termite mounds, but find that most of the snakes that inhabit these mounds are not species they want. This collecting method is very destructive.

Seeing snakes in the wild, especially in game reserves, is usually a matter of chance. Many snakes bask in the sun in the early mornings, so look on the eastern side of shrubs and bushes. If tree-living snakes occur in the region, check the lower branches of trees or look in shrubs, again on the eastern side early in the morning. Snakes are not easy to spot as they are secretive and elusive, and do their utmost to avoid humans. Should you come across a snake eating, especially a python with a large meal, observe it from a safe distance, as the snake will either leave its food or regurgitate it should you disturb it.

Graham Alexander

Snakes are extremely secretive and will disappear down the closest hole when disturbed.

SNAKE IDENTIFICATION

TO IDENTIFY A SNAKE, CAREFULLY CONSIDER THE FOLLOWING CHARACTERISTICS:

1. **SIZE.** Note the length of the snake, bearing in mind that short snakes may be hatchlings or juveniles of longer species.
2. **THICKNESS.** Check the snake's girth – is it thick- or thin-bodied? Most of the long, slender snakes are harmless, while thick-bodied snakes (with the exception of the Southern African Python) are often adders and are potentially dangerous.
3. **COLOUR AND MARKINGS.** Check if the snake is uniform in colour or whether it has markings from head to tail, or bars across its body. The majority of southern African snakes that have stripes or markings running down the body (from head to tail) are not considered dangerous to man, while most of the snakes that have bars running across the body are considered dangerous. Other snakes may have chevron-like markings down the back (Puff Adder), rhombic markings (Rhombic Egg-eater or Night Adder) or spots (Spotted Rock Snake or Variegated Bush Snake).
4. **HABITAT.** Many snakes are restricted to particular habitats and have fairly well-defined ranges. Check whether the habitat in which you find the snake corresponds with information in a field guide or a distribution map.
5. **ACTIVITY.** Take note of the time of day, as well as the weather conditions. Some snakes are active only in the day, while others move about exclusively at night. However, some nocturnal snakes may also move about at twilight and on overcast days; others that move mainly at night may occasionally bask in the sun.
6. **BEHAVIOUR.** Snakes react differently to the presence of perceived danger: some coil back into a striking position while hissing; others spread a hood; and some simply move off quickly. Nocturnal snakes tend to be relatively slow-moving, while most tree-living snakes disappear quickly into the closest tree or shrub.

Snake biology

Shedding

Hatchlings shed their skin soon after hatching. The outer layer of skin never grows or expands, and as the snake gets too big for it (or if it is damaged), a new layer of skin forms beneath it and the old layer is shed. In most instances the entire skin is shed in one piece, including the caps that cover the eyes. The snake will rub its nose against a rough surface such as a rock or log, and then virtually crawl out of the old skin. In large snakes the skin will often come off in pieces. Juvenile snakes grow fast and will shed their skins quite often – up to 15 times a year. As snakes get older, they shed less often, with large adults shedding only two or three times a year. A week or two prior to shedding, the eyes become a milky colour and it is said that the snake is 'in the blue'.

Snakes have either smooth or keeled scales, depending on the species. Cobras and mambas, as well as sand snakes and house snakes, have smooth scales, whereas most adders, the Boomslang and the Rinkhals have keeled scales.

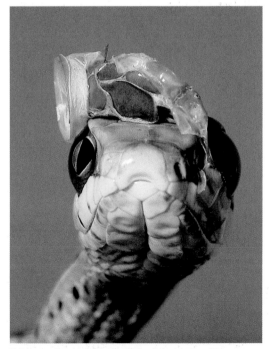

When snakes slough, they shed the entire skin, including the caps that cover their eyes.

Vision

Most snakes have good eyesight and are quick to escape when spotting an approaching person. It is thought that the Boomslang and vine snakes have far better vision than other snakes. However, even with their good vision, they tend to ignore stationary objects. If a night adder chases after a jumping toad and the toad freezes, the snake will often lose sight of the toad and will make use of its tongue to locate the prey.

Smell

Although snakes have nostrils, they use their tongues for smelling. The forked tongue picks up particles in the air and transfers them to a special organ in the roof of the mouth known as the Jacobson's organ. This method of smelling is very effective. It is often incorrectly thought that a snake may use its tongue to 'sting' or harm humans, but the tongue is perfectly harmless.

Hearing

As snakes have no external ear holes, they cannot hear airborne sound but are very sensitive to vibrations. Researchers working on Southern African Pythons struggle to get within 30 m of basking specimens, no matter how softly they approach. Their vibrations are easily picked up and the snakes disappear down their burrows.

Teeth and fangs

The majority of snakes have teeth, either small or large, that are used to capture prey and to assist with swallowing. A Brown House Snake, for example, will first use its sharp teeth to secure a rodent and, after constricting it, will further use them to push the prey into its extended jaws and down its throat. The snake will move its left row of upper teeth forward, followed by the right row, and continue alternating in this way until it has swallowed the entire creature – usually head first.

As egg-eaters eat only eggs and have no purpose for teeth, their teeth are greatly reduced and virtually non-existent. Wolf snakes, on the other hand, are small snakes but prey on smooth-bodied lizards: they require large teeth to penetrate the bodies of their prey. The Southern African Python has very strong, large, recurved teeth to secure large mammalian prey like antelope.

Some snakes have developed fangs and venom, although of those that do not have fangs, some do, nevertheless, appear to have venom. Venom consists of various proteins and is produced as modified saliva. A snake without fangs, but possessing venom, can inject its prey with venom simply by biting it.

Despite popular belief, the forked tongue of a snake cannot harm or sting and is used purely for smelling.

How do snakes eat?
Snakes cannot chew their food and must swallow it whole, even very large prey. Most non-venomous snakes constrict their catch and, in the process, do a considerable amount of muscle damage to the prey, which assists in digestion. Venomous snakes, on the other hand, use venom both to immobilize the prey and to assist digestion. The venom helps by breaking up the prey from within, thereby speeding up the digestive process.

Snake behaviour

Snakes are secretive creatures that spend most of their lives hiding in holes, rock crevices, hollow tree trunks or underground, emerging only to hunt for food or to bask in the sun. Some species rely on their excellent camouflage to escape detection. Most snakes are quick to flee when disturbed, and, far from seeking confrontation with people, prefer to disappear down the closest hole or into vegetation. Some snakes are active hunters, while others are ambush hunters, waiting patiently for a meal to pass by. Some species, like the Gaboon Adder, can lie in an ambush position for several months without moving much, deprived of food for that period but also not wasting any energy.

Because of their elusive lifestyles, snakes are not often seen, and it is estimated that even researchers on the lookout for snakes seldom encounter more than 5% of the specimens in any given area.

Most snakes become less active in winter, with some going into a state of torpor, depending on temperature. This is commonly referred to as 'hibernation', which is incorrect in our context as southern African snakes do not become totally inactive during winter as is implied by the term. Many species, while in a state of torpor during winter, will still emerge to bask in the sun on a hot winter's day. The majority of snakes avoid the heat of the day in summer, when temperatures may be lethal. Snakes frequent water and like to drink.

Diurnal or nocturnal

The majority of snakes are either more or less exclusively diurnal (active in the day) or nocturnal (active at night), although some nocturnal snakes move about in the day, especially on overcast days, while some diurnal snakes may also hunt or move about at night, especially when it is hot and humid after rain.

Diurnal snakes include the sand and grass snakes, mambas, several cobras and the green bush snakes, to mention a few. Some leave their hideouts to hunt early in the morning, thereby avoiding the heat of the day; others, like the sand snakes, can be seen foraging throughout the day. Many of the diurnal snakes tend to have round pupils, while a vertical pupil is often more advantageous for nocturnal snakes as it can be opened up to allow more light to enter the eyes.

Nocturnal snakes often start moving at twilight and tend to be most active till about 23h00. Most of southern Africa's adders, some cobras, tiger snakes and Brown House Snakes are active at night.

'Hibernation'

As snakes are cold-blooded, or poikilothermic, they cannot control their body temperature and have to rely on the environment for their body heat. They are ingenious at harnessing heat. A snake will bask in the morning sun with most of its body at an angle to the sun, sometimes even with the body flattened to increase its surface area. As the snake reaches its optimum body temperature, it will change its position to absorb less heat or it will move into the shade.

In winter, when there is insufficient sunlight to warm snakes adequately, they go into a state of torpor, often (incorrectly) referred to as 'hibernation'. During this period, snakes remain underground or in rock

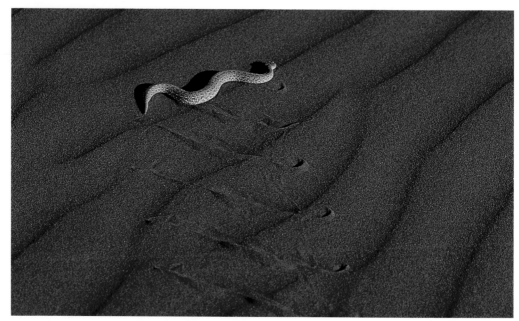

Péringuey's Adder sidewinds on the unstable dune sand.

crevices for long periods of time – up to six months or even more. They may come out to bask for a while, but, as a rule, they do not eat during this period. Several snakes of the same or different species can often be found seeking shelter under the same rock or in the same termite mound.

Locomotion

Snakes move in a few well-defined ways, and the majority of them can swim well. The most common method of locomotion is the normal serpentine manner – moving quickly in 'S'-movements. Snakes usually resort to this when escaping or when chasing fast-moving prey, such as lizards. Large snakes, like the Puff Adder, sometimes move very slowly in a straight line, using the 'caterpillar mode'. The ribs move the belly scales, thereby advancing the entire length of the snake steadily forwards. In a tree, a snake will often extend its body into the air, hook its head around a branch, and pull the body closer. Small desert adders sidewind, throwing one half of the body sideways followed by the other half. Sidewinding is beneficial when negotiating soft desert sand, which collapses easily. It also allows the snake to keep most of its body off the hot surface most of the time.

Reproduction

In the breeding season, females leave behind a scent trail, which males follow. Once a male has tracked down a mate, he crawls onto the female, inspects her with his flickering tongue, and then uses one of his two penises, known as the hemipenes, to copulate. For this purpose, a penis is everted, or turned inside out, and copulation can last for a couple of hours.

The majority of snakes are egg-laying or **oviparous**. The female seeks a suitable, well-protected, damp spot, like a hollow tree trunk, log or deserted termite mound in which to lay her eggs. The clutch varies from as few as two to well over 60 eggs, depending on the species. The eggs are usually white and soft with a leathery texture. The majority of snakes abandon their eggs after laying them, the Southern African Python and Rhombic Skaapstekers being exceptions. These snakes remain with their eggs throughout incubation and protect them. Once the young are ready to hatch, they use their egg-tooth – a dry, sharp piece of skin on the tip of the nose – to cut the egg from the inside. Newly hatched snakes can survive on absorbed yolk for the first few weeks. Newborn snakes are often perfect replicas of the adults.

Some snakes produce live young and are referred to as **viviparous**. This is not true live birth as occurs in mammals. The female develops eggs within her body and lays them just before they are due to hatch. The young are covered in a fine membrane that is easily ruptured. The advantage of this form of reproduction is that the female does not abandon her eggs and can bask in the sun to assist with incubation.

What is the most venomous or dangerous snake?
People often wonder which southern African snake is
the most venomous or dangerous. The Boomslang (right),
drop for drop, has the most potent venom of any African snake,
and a minute drop can kill a human. Fortunately, this snake has
small quantities of venom and is extremely docile. It seldom strikes,
and most victims tend to be snake handlers. The most dangerous snake in
the region, however, is the Black Mamba, due to its size (sometimes exceeding 4 m in
length), nervous disposition and the large quantities of potent neurotoxic venom it produces.
This snake will not hesitate to strike when cornered or threatened.

Venomous and dangerous snakes

The majority of the region's snakes are not considered dangerous to humans; in fact, only about 10%
are thought to be so. Most snakes have no fangs nor venom, or minute fangs and mild venom that is of
little consequence to man.

Snakes without fangs and venom, like the Brown House Snake or the Common Brown Water Snake,
do have teeth, and will draw blood if they bite. But the teeth, though sharp, are tiny, and deliver a bite
that feels like the prick of a small thorn. Some of the harmless snakes can inflict bites that are very painful, though not lethal. The Mole Snake, for instance, has very strong, sharp teeth and moves its head up
and down when biting, like the action of a tin opener; such bites could require stitches. The Southern
African Python may exceed 5 m in length, and such a large snake can inflict an extremely painful bite
that may result in the victim requiring many stitches, such as when bitten by a dog. Instances of pythons
attacking people are rare, and there are only two or three cases of people being killed by large pythons
in Africa during the last two centuries.

Several snakes have developed a venom apparatus and fangs to assist with feeding and, to a lesser
degree, for self-defence. Snakes like the Puff Adder will strike out quickly, inject their venom in a fraction
of a second, and then follow the prey's scent using their forked tongue. Other venomous snakes, like the
Boomslang, hang on to their prey while the venom slowly takes effect.

As a form of self-defence, venom is not very effective as it cannot kill a large animal or a human
within minutes. Some of the venomous snakes have adapted to spit their venom, which is far more effective than biting. Venom in an aggressor's eyes causes severe irritation and temporary blindness, allowing
the embattled snake to escape.

Venomous snakes are generally divided into three groups: snakes with short, primitive, grooved
back fangs situated roughly below the eyes (Boomslang, vine snakes, sand snakes, tiger snakes, Herald
Snake); those with short fixed fangs in the front of the mouth (mambas, cobras); and snakes with large,
moveable fangs in the front of the
mouth that fold back against the roof
of the mouth when not in use (Puff
Adder, dwarf adders, night adders). In
the latter two groups the fangs are hollow, like hypodermic needles, and the
venom comes from the venom glands at
the back of the upper jaw, which passes
down the hollow core of the fangs when
the snake bites.

Types of venom and effects

The composition of snake venom is
quite complex. There are three types of
venom: **haemotoxins**, **cytotoxins** and
neurotoxins. This is perhaps an over-
simplification, as most snakes have a
combination of these venoms.

The Puff Adder has large, moveable fangs.

The venom of the dangerous back-fanged snakes is predominantly haemotoxic, affecting the body's blood-clotting mechanism. The victim will experience internal bleeding, with dark patches appearing on the skin in the vicinity of the kidneys and, eventually, in the vicinity of the lungs. This venom acts slowly and can take more than a day or two before serious symptoms develop. Eventually a victim will bleed from the mouth, nose and ears and, in serious, untreated cases, death will follow as a result of brain haemorrhage.

Adders and some of the cobras like the Mozambique Spitting Cobra have predominantly cytotoxic or cell-destroying venoms that cause massive swelling, extreme pain, discoloration at the site of the bite and extensive tissue damage. In some instances secondary infection does further damage and victims may require limb amputation. Cytotoxic venom usually takes effect quite slowly, giving the victim sufficient time to get proper medical care. Puff Adders account for the greatest number of serious snakebite cases in southern Africa, but the mortality rate is low.

The mambas and most cobras have a neurotoxic or nerve-destroying venom. The venom is quickly absorbed and fast acting, affecting the central nervous system. Symptoms include difficulty in breathing, dizziness and loss of consciousness. In untreated serious cases the victims stop breathing and die from a lack of oxygen to the brain. As these venoms act quickly, victims will need urgent medical care.

Which snakes account for the most human deaths?

Very few human deaths from snakebite are recorded annually in southern Africa, with a figure of around 10 fatalities per annum usually quoted. Most of these deaths are caused by bites from Cape Cobras and Black Mambas, and the majority of bites with serious consequences are inflicted by the Puff Adder. Other snakes that are occasionally responsible for fatalities include the Snouted Cobra and the Mozambique Spitting Cobra.

Black Mamba

Puff Adder

Cape Cobra

Mozambique Spitting Cobra

SNAKEBITE

Of the 151 snake species in southern Africa, around 16 are considered dangerous to humans. Fewer than 10 deaths as a result of snakebite are reported annually in South Africa; the majority of snakebite victims survive. Snakebite serum is not considered a first aid measure and should ideally be administered by doctors in a hospital environment.

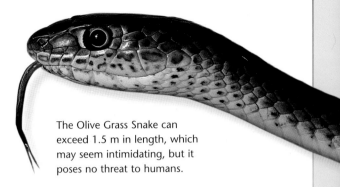

The Olive Grass Snake can exceed 1.5 m in length, which may seem intimidating, but it poses no threat to humans.

FIRST AID MEASURES

DO

- Keep the victim calm. Reassure them by explaining that few snakebites are serious and that treatment is usually effective.
- Immobilize the victim. Activity may speed up the circulation of venom around the body. Elevate the site of the bite to restrict blood flow and the spread of venom.
- Apply a crepe bandage or pressure bandage to the bitten limb. The bandage should be applied from the site of the bite towards the trunk of the body; it should slow down the lymphatic system but not restrict blood circulation.
- Avoid applying a tourniquet except in the case of a bite from a mamba or cobra. Even then, a tourniquet should only be considered if you are an experienced first aider. Cutting off blood supply may result in the victim losing a limb.
- Resort to 'mouth to mouth' resuscitation if the victim experiences difficulty in breathing or ceases breathing. This could be life-saving and should be maintained until medical care is obtained.
- Transport the victim to a hospital as soon as possible. The sooner the victim receives proper medical care, the better their chances of complete recovery.

DON'T

- Attempt to kill the snake for identification purposes – a second bite would complicate matters. The hospital staff will treat the victim's symptoms.
- Cut near the site of the bite, and avoid ineffective treatment like Condy's crystals, massive doses of vitamins or shock therapy.
- Inject anti-snakebite serum unless the bite is from a Black Mamba or Cape Cobra and you are familiar with the intravenous administration of such serum and the potential after-effects. Even then, it is better for a qualified person to administer the serum.

VENOM IN THE EYES

- Rinse the affected eye with large quantities of water.
- Do not rub the eye.
- There is no evidence that milk, beer or urine is more effective than water. You are not trying to neutralize the venom, merely to dilute it.
- Do not use diluted anti-snakebite serum. Rather transport the victim to a doctor or hospital.
- Do not try to kill or capture the snake. The identification of the snake is not important.
- Reassure the victim – their eyes should recover fully within a few days.

PREVENTING SNAKEBITE

- Wear hiking boots and denim trousers in the field.
- If you come across a snake, do not attempt to catch or kill it. Move away from it; snakes do not follow or chase people.
- Be careful when collecting firewood and do not put your hands where you can't see them.
- Keep your property clear of building rubble and other potential shelters such as sheets of corrugated roofing. These may attract rodents and toads, as well as snakes.

Large Adders

There are three common adders in southern Africa: the Puff Adder, Gaboon Adder and Berg Adder. These snakes are active at night, but may bask during the day. Adders have large fangs in the front of the mouth that fold back against the roof of the mouth when not in use. When the snake strikes, the fangs are quickly folded forward and are darted into the victim. Most adder venoms are predominantly cell-destroying, causing severe pain, discoloration of the skin and necrosis (death of cells).

▲
The Puff Adder has strongly keeled scales, like most southern African adders.

Some believe that the Puff Adder only strikes backwards. This is not true – like other snakes, it strikes forwards or to the side. It may turn around and strike in the opposite direction, but it is not able to strike backwards.

▲
The fangs of the Puff Adder may exceed 20 mm in length. They fold back against the roof of the mouth when not in use.

▲
Puff Adders are ambush hunters and will remain in one position for days, waiting for prey to pass.

The **Puff Adder** reaches an average length of just under a metre, but may exceed 1.5 m. This fat and robust adder has a triangular head distinct from the body, and is covered in strongly keeled scales. It is by far the most common adder in southern Africa and is found throughout most of the region, except for evergreen forests and true deserts. This snake lives on the ground in a variety of habitats. Its diet consists largely of rodents. Females give birth to between 20 and 40 young at a time. It is a popular fallacy that the young eat their way out of the mother's uterus. The Puff Adder is a very dangerous snake as it relies on its perfect camouflage to avoid danger. It will remain motionless and will only hiss and strike out viciously if someone stands on it or very close to it. It has very large fangs and accounts for the majority of serious snakebite cases in South Africa. This is a slow-moving, bad-tempered snake that should never be approached.

Though a slow mover, the Puff Adder will disappear quickly if disturbed, with characteristic serpentine-like movement.

Puff Adders from KwaZulu-Natal tend to be more brightly coloured than those found further inland.

Several of the nocturnal snakes, including the Puff Adder, have a slit pupil.

When threatened, the Puff Adder will draw its head back into a striking position.

Tell-tale signs

- Bulky snakes with triangular head distinct from the rest of the body
- Keeled scales on the body
- Usually found on the ground
- Fond of basking in the sun
- Will huff and puff when threatened

The chevron markings down the back are a characteristic of the Puff Adder.

Warren Schmidt

The Gaboon Adder has the largest fangs of any venomous snake in the world.

The **Gaboon Adder** is the biggest adder in southern Africa and may exceed 1.6 m in length. It is a beautifully coloured snake with a large, light, triangular head and bulky body. This adder is a forest dweller that seldom moves and may remain in the same position for several days, where it awaits its prey in ambush. The Gaboon Adder feeds on rodents, but can take large prey such as monkeys or small duikers. Females produce up to 30 young in summer. This is a bad-tempered snake that hisses and puffs when threatened. Its fangs are the largest of any African snake, and may exceed 40 mm in length. With its potent venom and enormous venom glands, the Gaboon Adder is capable of inflicting a very serious bite, often with fatal results.

The Gaboon Adder is perfectly camouflaged and extremely difficult to see, especially in dense jungle habitat.

The head of a large Gaboon Adder is larger than a person's hand.

Within southern Africa, the Gaboon Adder is found only in northern KwaZulu-Natal and eastern Zimbabwe. Large parts of its habitat have been destroyed, especially in northern KwaZulu-Natal, where informal settlements have developed, destroying most of the Dukuduku Forest. The exact status of this snake is not known, and research is currently under way to assess the situation.

The **Berg Adder** is a smaller adder, reaching a maximum length of around 600 mm. The head is triangular and distinct from the rest of the body, typical of most adders. As its common name indicates, it prefers mountainous regions and occurs in the Western and southern Cape, the KwaZulu-Natal Drakensberg, Mpumalanga and eastern Zimbabwe. Its diet consists of lizards and small rodents, but amphibians are also taken. Between 4 and 16 young, measuring 90–150 mm, are produced in late summer. It is a bad-tempered snake that puffs and hisses if confronted and will readily strike. Mountaineers and hikers are at risk, as it often basks in footpaths and on rocky ledges where it is well camouflaged. Fortunately, the venom appears to be relatively mild and no fatal bites have been reported.

▲
This brightly coloured Berg Adder is found in the Western Cape.

This dull Berg Adder from Mpumalanga province shows faint markings.
▼

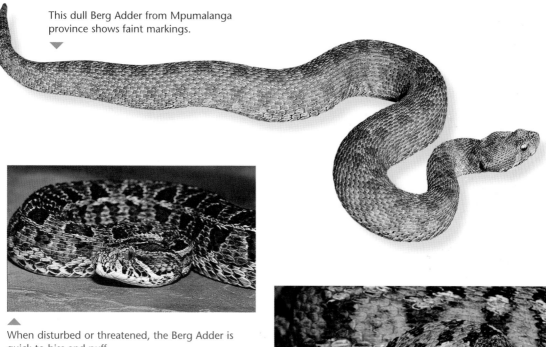

▲
When disturbed or threatened, the Berg Adder is quick to hiss and puff.

▲
Mountain climbers are at risk of being bitten, as Berg Adders often bask on rock faces, out of sight.

▲
The Berg Adder has fairly mild venom, and no fatal bites have been recorded.

Dwarf Adders

▲
A dull greyish-brown Horned Adder from Namibia.

There are seven dwarf adders that occur largely in the drier, western half of the region. They average around 250–350 mm in length and have triangular heads that are well distinguished from the rest of the body. Their venom is largely cell-destroying, and their bite is rather painful but seldom life-threatening.

The **Horned Adder** usually has a single, distinct horn above each eye. Individuals vary in colour, usually depending on the area in which they occur. This is the most common of the dwarf adders with the widest distribution, covering much of the western half of southern Africa, but extending as far east as Mpumalanga and Zimbabwe. It seeks shelter in the shade of shrubs, and emerges in the early evening to hunt for lizards. It feeds on small lizards such as geckos and skinks, as well as small birds, rodents and frogs. Between 3 and 8, but as many as 27, young are produced in summer or early autumn. When threatened, a Horned Adder will inflate its body, hiss loudly and strike repeatedly.

▲
The horns of this snake are not always very large. This specimen shows reduced horns.

◀ This reddish Horned Adder was found on similar-coloured sand in the Kalahari.

The dwarf adders all look fairly similar and it's hard to distinguish one from another. A bite from any one of the small adders may be extremely painful and result in some swelling, especially those on the finger, but the symptoms are mild and seldom of any serious concern.

The **Many-horned Adder** is probably the largest of the dwarf adders, with captive individuals reaching a length of 750 mm. It occurs in the drier west and usually has a tuft of around five or six horns above each eye. This snake prefers rocky areas and is very common around Springbok in Namaqualand. During the day it seeks shelter in rodent burrows and rock cracks and emerges at sunset to hunt for lizards and small rodents. Between 4 and 14 young, measuring 130–160 mm, are produced in late summer. Though the bite of this snake is not thought to be life-threatening, it is usually extremely painful.

The **Desert Mountain Adder** is a rare snake with a triangular head and dull grey appearance. It is found on dry, rocky hillsides in the vicinity of the Orange River, close to or in the Richtersveld, and a little further inland. This snake is very well camouflaged and difficult to see. It doesn't bury itself in sand like some of the other little adders, and hisses and strikes if cornered. Females produce up to 5 young in summer.

The Many-horned Adder is the largest of the dwarf adders, reaching a length of 750 mm.

The Desert Mountain Adder has rather dull coloration and is well camouflaged among rocks and stones.

The Many-horned Adder has little clusters of horns above each eye. ▶

◀ The Desert Mountain Adder has no horns above the eyes.

Tell-tale signs

- Triangular head, very distinct from the rest of the body
- Some have a single horn or tufts of horns above the eyes
- Most active at sunset or in the early morning
- Hiss and puff and strike aggressively if threatened
- Often seen crossing roads at night

Graham Alexander

The Plain Mountain Adder is currently listed as Vulnerable in the latest South African Red Data Book.

Marius Burger

The Red Adder lacks horns above the eyes.

The **Plain Mountain Adder** is dull reddish brown in colour, but may have faint darker blotches on the back. It is found only in the Sneeuberg, from north of Graaff-Reinet to Cradock. It hides under rocks or in grass tussocks during the day, but may emerge to bask in the sun. It is a rare little adder that feeds on lizards and small rodents. Up to 8 young are produced in summer. Although no human bites have been recorded to date, the venom of this snake is probably similar to that of other small adders.

The **Red Adder** is plain red or reddish-brown with paired blotches on the back. It occurs from the Cederberg to the Roggeveldberg and Komsberg, in the same areas as the Many-horned Adder. It hides under shrubs and rocks, but may bask in the mornings. This rare adder was first described in 1997. It feeds on lizards, especially geckos and skinks, as well as small rodents. Up to 10 young are born in summer. No human bites have been recorded, but the venom of this snake is thought to be similar to that of the other small adders, causing local pain and swelling.

Marius Burger

This rare little adder, the Red Adder, was described as recently as 1997.

The **Albany Adder** is found only in the Algoa Bay area of the Eastern Cape, where most of its habitat has been destroyed. Further development in the area will pose a serious threat to the survival of this species. Very few individuals have ever been seen and little is known of the habits of this snake.

The **Southern Adder** grows in excess of 400 mm and has little tufts of horns above each eye that are greatly reduced and smaller than those of the Many-horned Adder. It occurs in low-lying coastal fynbos in the southwestern Cape. It has been found seeking shelter under limestone rock slabs and is most active in the early mornings or evenings. Like the other small adders, it feeds on lizards and small rodents. Up to 7 young are produced in summer.

Marius Burger

The Albany Adder occurs exclusively in the Algoa Bay area of the Eastern Cape.

Tony Phelps

The Southern Adder occurs in low-lying coastal fynbos in the southwestern Cape.

Dune Adders

Two species of dune adder inhabit the arid west coast of southern Africa, where they are uniquely adapted to survive in extreme sandy conditions. They are small adders with heads distinct from the rest of the body, and with body patterns and colours that blend in well with their environment. They obtain moisture from their food and by drinking water that condenses on their bodies when fog moves in from the cold Atlantic Ocean. Both dune adders burrow into loose sand, often leaving only the eyes exposed to see predators and prey. They also have the unique ability to sidewind in soft sand, throwing one half of the body sideways, followed by the other half. This enables them to move on unstable, often collapsing, dune sand and also to keep most of the body off the hot sand. These dune adders are threatened by habitat destruction resulting from alluvial diamond mining, as well as by recreational vehicles, especially quad bikes.

▲
The Namaqua Dwarf Adder is the smallest adder in the world.

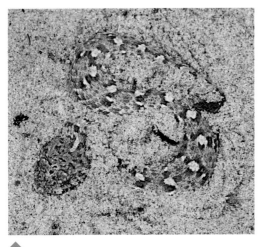

▲
A Namaqua Dwarf Adder half buried in the sand, awaiting prey in ambush.

▲
Dune adders leave very distinct tracks in the soft dune sand.

The Namaqua Dwarf Adder lacks horns, and its eyes are situated very high up on the head, enabling it to see when buried in sand.
▼

▲
Péringuey's Adder has a flat, triangular head that is distinct from the rest of its body.

The eyes of Péringuey's Adder are situated on top of the head, allowing the snake to see when completely buried in sand.

The **Namaqua Dwarf Adder** is the world's smallest adder, averaging a mere 200 mm. Its coloration is greyish brown with blotches, allowing it to blend well into the environment. The eyes are situated high up on the sides of the head. This snake is found along the coast from Little Namaqualand to Lüderitz Bay in Namibia. Like most other small adders, it is largely active at night but basks in the morning. It leaves a distinct track in the loose sand that criss-crosses from one shrub to the next, with regular intervals where the snake may shuffle into the sand. The Namaqua Dwarf Adder feeds on lizards, which are usually bitten and held while the venom takes effect. Up to 7 minute young are produced in summer. Though venomous, this desert adder has a minute yield of mild venom and poses no threat to humans.

Péringuey's Adder averages 250 mm, and is fat with a flat, triangular head that is very distinct from the rest of the body. The eyes are situated on top of the head. This snake occurs along the west coast, from southern Namibia into Angola. This little adder buries itself in sand and awaits its prey in ambush: only the eyes and the dark tip of its tail remain exposed, the latter being used as a lure to attract lizards. Like the Namaqua Dwarf Adder, this snake also shuffles itself into loose sand and sidewinds, often leaving distinct S-shaped markings in the sand. Females produce up to 10 young in summer.

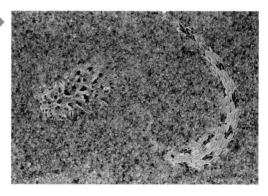

▲
A Péringuey's Adder sidewinding over the hot, unstable dune sand.

Like many other snakes, both dune adders are illegally collected for the pet trade and many are illegally exported. They seldom do well in captivity because of their specialized requirements, including a dry environment and a specific diet. Fortunately, both snakes occur largely in protected and restricted areas.

Tell-tale signs

- Small and stubby
- Rounded, flattened head distinct from the rest of the body
- Lack horns above the eyes
- Eyes very high up on the sides of the head or on top of the head
- Often burrow into loose sand

Night Adders

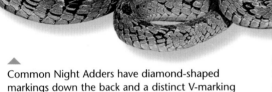

Unlike the other adders in the region, night adders are slender snakes with a head that is barely distinct from the rest of the body. These snakes also differ in that they lay eggs, whereas all the other adders produce live young. Furthermore, they have the longest venom glands of any of the region's snakes – extending down into the neck region. Two species of night adder occur largely in the wetter eastern half of southern Africa, including much of Zimbabwe and northern Botswana.

The **Common Night Adder** reaches a length of around 1 m. It has dark blotches down the body and is easily identified by a distinct dark V-marking on the head that extends backwards from between the eyes. This snake is found

▲
Common Night Adders have diamond-shaped markings down the back and a distinct V-marking on the head.

▲
Most southern African adders give birth to live young, but the Common Night Adder lays eggs.

▲
Though largely nocturnal, Common Night Adders also hunt on overcast days.

Warren Schmidt

▲
Night adders feed on frogs and toads and frequent damp localities.

▲
The Snouted Night Adder is very similar to the Common Night Adder but is much smaller.

◀ The V-marking is distinct on the head of this Snouted Night Adder.

▲
The Snouted Night Adder has an upturned snout, hence the common name.

throughout most of the eastern half of the region, as well as in the wetter parts of northern Botswana. Like most adders, the night adder is largely active at night but is also often found hunting for food on overcast days. Otherwise, it hides among stones and logs, in termite mounds and among building rubble. It is regularly found near houses, where it hunts for frogs and toads. It is not as bad-tempered as most adders and is quick to retreat if disturbed. If provoked, it will inflate its body and hiss loudly. The cytotoxic venom, though fairly potent and often resulting in painful bites, is not considered deadly to humans. Females lay up to 26 eggs as often as three times in summer.

The **Snouted Night Adder** is easily confused with the Common Night Adder as it is very similar in appearance and has the distinct, dark V-marking on the head. This adder is smaller, however, reaching a maximum length of around 400 mm. It also differs in having an upturned snout, hence the common name. Its distribution is limited to the wetter eastern parts of Limpopo, Mpumalanga, Swaziland and KwaZulu-Natal, as well as much of Zimbabwe. The Snouted Night Adder is a specialized feeder that preys on frogs and toads. It lays between 3 and 9 eggs in summer, with the young measuring 100 mm in length. The venom is feebly cytotoxic and may cause pain and swelling but is not considered dangerous to humans.

Night adders are known to engage in male combat. Individuals will raise their heads and attempt to push their adversaries to the ground in a sort of wrestling match. Many different snake species are known to engage in male combat – the males often twisting their bodies around one another. Very few snakes will actually bite during male combat, the Mole Snake being an exception.

Tell-tale signs

- Head barely distinct from the rest of the body
- Distinct, dark V-marking extending from between the eyes to the back of the head
- Medium-sized eyes with round pupils
- Most active at night
- Frequent damp localities
- Found on the ground

Mambas

The Black Mamba is notorious for lifting the front third of its body well off the ground.

The head of the Black Mamba is commonly described as being 'coffin-shaped'.

There are two mambas in southern Africa, the Black Mamba and the Green Mamba. It is sometimes incorrectly said that the Green Mamba eventually becomes a Black Mamba with age. The two are, in fact, quite different in appearance and behaviour. Both these snakes are extremely dangerous, as they possess a potent neurotoxic or nerve-destroying venom that can quickly affect the central nervous system. After a bite the onset of symptoms may be dramatic, and it is vitally important that the victim is hospitalized as soon as possible. Large quantities of antivenom may be required to save the victim's life. The Black Mamba is often considered the most dangerous snake in the world. Mambas are diurnal snakes, being active during the day and sleeping at night.

The **Black Mamba** is the largest venomous snake in Africa, averaging around 3 m but with a maximum length of almost 4.5 m. This snake is usually greyish-brown to olive-brown or gunmetal-grey with a lighter belly, but old adults may be black. The Black Mamba is widely distributed in southern Africa and is found from the Eastern Cape through KwaZulu-Natal, Swaziland, Mpumalanga, parts of Gauteng, Limpopo and North West province into Zimbabwe, Botswana, and central and northern Namibia. It lives in termite mounds, rock outcrops, hollow tree trunks and animal burrows

When cornered, the Black Mamba will gape, exposing the black interior of its mouth.

Despite its name, the Black Mamba is seldom black in colour – it is usually a greyish brown to gunmetal grey and may darken with age.

in the ground. Despite popular belief, the Black Mamba is not aggressive but rather very nervous. If disturbed, it will always try to escape, but if cornered it may gape, exposing the black lining of the mouth, and will not hesitate to strike. Stories of men on horseback being chased by Black Mambas are not true – the maximum speed of the fastest snake is probably similar to the speed of a marathon runner. Snakes also cannot maintain a high speed for any length of time and tire quickly. This snake feeds on mammals such as rats, tree squirrels, dassies, birds and snakes. Between 6 and 17 eggs are laid in summer. The young measure 400–600 mm in length, growing up to 2 m within a year.

The Green Mamba's eyes are olive green, not golden like some green snakes.

The **Green Mamba** is smaller, averaging a length of 1.8 m. As the name indicates, it is bright emerald-green above and may have a few scattered yellow scales on the body. The belly is usually pale green and the eye is olive-green, never golden-orange like some of the green bush snakes. It has a restricted distribution within the region and is largely confined to thick coastal bush and forest close to the sea, from the Eastern Cape through KwaZulu-Natal into Mozambique and eastern Zimbabwe. The Green Mamba spends most of its time in trees and feeds largely on birds, their young and tree-living mammals, including bats. Between 6 and 17 eggs are produced, and the young measure 300–450 mm in length. The venom is extremely potent and deadly. Fortunately, few people are bitten by this snake.

A Green Mamba about to hatch. Hatchlings of venomous species such as this are dangerous the moment they emerge.

Warren Schmidt

Green Mambas are largely tree-living but may descend to the ground to bask or to hunt for food.

The myth about a snake that moves quickly through bush with a whistling sound and a feather on its head was probably initiated by the sighting of a Black Mamba with a piece of shed skin stuck to its head. The speed of snakes is grossly exaggerated, as they move slower than a marathon runner.

Tell-tale signs

- Coffin-shaped head
- Medium to large eyes with a round pupil
- Active during the day
- May be found in shrubs, trees or thick bush or on the ground
- Will move quickly if disturbed

Non-spitting Cobras

There are four non-spitting cobras in southern Africa. They all have potent neurotoxic or nerve-destroying venom that, in the event of snakebite, can prove fatal if not treated quickly. Cobras are active largely in the day but are often found in fowl runs or bird aviaries at night. They have broad heads that are barely distinct from the rest of the body and fairly large eyes with round pupils. These snakes all spread a hood when cornered. The head is raised off the ground and the ribs in the neck region are pushed out to the sides to form the hood. This is done to intimidate predators by making the snake appear larger.

The **Cape Cobra** averages around 1.2 m, seldom exceeding 1.6 m in length. It varies in colour from very dark to light, and may have speckles with shades of light brown and orange in between. The Cape Cobra is found largely in the Cape but extends into Namibia, Botswana and the Free State. It is very active during the day and early evenings when it hunts for food, even climbing into trees. Females lay up to 20 eggs in summer. When attacked, it will stand its ground and spread an impressive hood, striking readily. The venom is highly neurotoxic and the Cape Cobra accounts for the most human deaths resulting from snakebite in South Africa. It feeds on rodents and birds, as well as other snakes.

Warren Schmidt

▲ The Cape Cobra actively hunts for food during the day. It prefers rodents and birds but will also eat other snakes.

◀ Cape Cobras vary in colour from black to brown, orange, yellow or cream, and may be speckled. Juveniles usually have a dark band in the region of the throat.

Warren Schmidt

▲ A speckled Cape Cobra in a defensive pose, spreading a hood.

The **Snouted Cobra**, formerly known as the Egyptian Cobra, is one of southern Africa's largest cobras, reaching a length of 2.6 m. It is usually a greyish-brown to dark brown snake, but banded individuals are encountered in some areas. This snake occurs from KwaZulu-Natal into Swaziland, Mpumalanga, Limpopo, North West, eastern Botswana and Zimbabwe. It is a robust snake that often inhabits a permanent home, which may be a rodent burrow, hollow log or termite mound, for many years. This snake is more active in the evenings and will begin hunting for rodents, birds and other snakes at dusk. It is known for raiding poultry runs at night for chicks and eggs. Females produce up to 33 eggs in early summer. Large individuals are known to lift as much as half of their bodies off the ground when confronted, while spreading an impressive hood. Fortunately, they usually disappear down the nearest hole if given the opportunity. A bite from a large Snouted Cobra will result in alarming symptoms and will require urgent medical attention.

Warren Schmidt

The Snouted Cobra is usually quite shy and retiring, but spreads an impressive hood when cornered.

Warren Schmidt

The Snouted Cobra is one of southern Africa's largest cobras, reaching a length of almost 3 m.

Most Snouted Cobras are greyish-brown, but banded individuals occur throughout its range.

Cape Cobras often raid Sociable Weaver nests. The snake will climb into the tree and probe various openings in the massive nest in search of birds, ignoring those mobbing it while it searches. Several young and eggs will be eaten in such a session.

Tell-tale signs

- Medium to large eyes with round pupils
- Body has smooth, shiny appearance
- Found mainly on the ground, but climb into trees and shrubs
- Active during the day and in the early evenings
- Lift head off the ground and spread a hood when threatened
- Do not spit venom

Colin Tilbury

Anchieta's Cobra is very similar to the Snouted Cobra in behaviour but tends to be more aggressive if threatened. It is a smaller snake, averaging around 1 m in length. Anchieta's Cobra occurs in northern Namibia and northern Botswana. Like the Snouted Cobra, it is also often found in poultry runs, where it swallows eggs whole. It also feeds on rodents, birds, toads and other snakes. Anchieta's Cobra lays eggs in summer; the young measure 220–340 mm.

Colin Tilbury

▲
Like all southern African cobras, Anchieta's Cobra is quick to spread a defensive hood when cornered or threatened.

Anchieta's Cobra is found in the northern parts of Namibia and Botswana, and further north. ▶

Colin Tilbury

▲
Though largely ground-living, the Forest Cobra is also at home in shrubs and trees.

The **Forest Cobra** averages around 2 m, reaching a maximum length of 2.7 m, and is probably the largest cobra in Africa. It is usually yellow-brown on the forepart of the body, but darker brown to black towards the back. The polished scales give it a shiny appearance. It is usually found in closed-canopy coastal forest in northern KwaZulu-Natal. The Forest Cobra is a quick, alert snake that is at home in trees and shrubs as well as in water. It hunts in the evenings, but is fond of basking during the day. Its diet includes rodents, birds, toads and other snakes. Females lay up to 26 smooth white eggs. This snake possesses a potent neurotoxic or nerve-destroying venom, but avoids humans and is quick to disappear into the closest bush or shrub if disturbed.

When threatened, the Forest Cobra lifts as much as half of its body off the ground while spreading a narrow hood. ▶

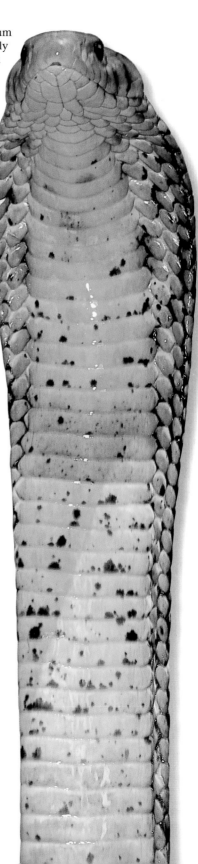

▲
The Forest Cobra has smooth, highly polished scales that give it a shiny appearance.

▲
The Forest Cobra is yellowish-brown with darker flecks, becoming much darker towards the tail.

Spitting Snakes

Warren Schmidt

Despite popular belief, very few snakes have the ability to spit or eject their venom. Spitting snakes have a hole near the tip of the fang pointing forwards rather than downwards, as is the case in other venomous snakes. These snakes apply pressure to the venom glands, which are situated towards the back of the upper jaw, and the venom is ejected forward. The spitting action is not as accurate as is often thought, but it is effective, as the droplets of venom are sprayed forward in the general direction of danger and will invariably end up in the target's eyes. Venom is ejected effectively up to a distance of about 3 m, and it is the same venom that would be injected in a bite.

The **Mozambique Spitting Cobra** or **M'fezi** averages around 1.2 m in length. This cobra is slate-grey to dark brown with a salmon-pink belly and blackish markings in the throat region, which are seen when the snake spreads a hood. It is one of the most common spitting snakes in the region, and is found in the wetter half of southern Africa, extending northwards into Zimbabwe, Botswana and northern Namibia. This snake may be seen foraging on overcast days, but is more active at night when it hunts for rodents, birds, lizards, toads and other snakes. It is a shy snake and is quick to escape if given the chance. If cornered, it will spread a hood and spit its venom. The venom supply of a spitting snake appears to be inexhaustible, and they can continue spitting effectively for a long time. The venom of the Mozambique Spitting Cobra is potently cytotoxic or cell-destroying, and bites are quite common, especially in KwaZulu-Natal. Urgent medical care is required in such an event. Females produce 10–22 eggs in midsummer; the young measure 230–250 mm.

◄ The Mozambique Spitting Cobra can both spit its venom or inject it by biting.

▲
The Mozambique Spitting Cobra usually spits while spreading a hood but can also spit without lifting its head.

The **Black-necked Spitting Cobra** averages 1.2–1.5 m in length and may be similar to the Mozambique Spitting Cobra in appearance, but much darker. It is only found in the Caprivi Strip in Namibia. The Black-necked Spitting Cobra lives in rodent burrows, deserted termite mounds or in hollow tree trunks. It hunts for food at night and feeds on a variety of prey including rodents, toads, birds and other snakes. When threatened or cornered it will spread a hood and spit venom. Between 10 and 22 eggs are produced in summer.

The **Black Spitting Cobra** may grow to lengths of more than 2 m. As the common name indicates, it is shiny black in colour. This snake is found from Little Namaqualand northwards into Namibia. It is often seen crossing roads during the day and may be confused with dark varieties of the Cape Cobra. In addition to rodents and birds, it favours snakes, including the Puff Adder, in its diet. When threatened, it spreads an impressive hood and spits very effectively. The venom of spitting cobras is dangerously cytotoxic or cell-destroying, and urgent medical care is required in the event of a bite. Between 10 and 22 eggs are produced.

The Black Spitting Cobra is a shiny black colour and may be confused with the black variety of the Cape Cobra, which cannot spit.

The Black-necked Spitting Cobra only just enters our range in the Caprivi Strip in northern Namibia.

Snake venom in the eyes is very painful – rather like getting a mixture of petrol and sand in your eyes. There are many fallacies about treating venom in the eyes. The best treatment is to rinse the eyes carefully with lots of running water. The aim is to dilute the venom in the eyes, not necessarily to neutralize it. Any bland liquid can be used, including beer, milk or even urine, but water is by far the best. It is probable that the victim will have inflamed eyes for a few days, and a visit to a doctor is recommended. Avoid using diluted antivenom to treat venom in the eyes.

Tell-tale signs

- Medium to large eyes with round pupils
- Smooth shiny body scales except for the Rinkhals
- Found mainly on the ground
- Active both during the day and at night
- Spread an impressive hood when cornered
- May play dead

The Zebra Cobra gets its common name from its banded appearance.

The **Zebra Cobra** is light grey-brown with 64–117 black bands on the body and tail, hence the common name. This snake occurs in northern Namibia and averages just over a metre in length. It is largely active at night and is often found crossing roads, resulting in large numbers of Zebra Cobras being killed by vehicles. Its diet consists of rodents, lizards, amphibians and snakes. This shy snake is quick to escape, but if necessary it will stand its ground, spread a hood and spit its venom. Between 10 and 22 eggs are produced.

A Zebra Cobra sunning itself on a rock, spreading a partial hood to absorb more heat.

When cornered, the Zebra Cobra will spread a hood, spitting effectively and continuously while under threat.

The **Rinkhals,** though closely related, is not a true cobra. There are some important skeletal differences, and it bears live young. There are two colour phases: a dark grey to black phase with two or three white bars in the throat region, and a banded version where the top of the body has light and dark bars across the back and tail. This snake is widespread over much of South Africa, except for the drier west, and is also found in eastern Zimbabwe. The Rinkhals is predominantly a grassland species that inhabits rodent burrows and is common on smallholdings. It is mainly active in the day and will often bask near its hole. Its diet consists of rodents, toads, other snakes, birds and their eggs. If cornered, this snake will spread a hood while lifting close to half its body off the ground. It only spits from a reared position, throwing the front third of the body forward when spitting. Like some other snakes, the Rinkhals also plays dead. It will turn part of its body upside down, sometimes with the mouth agape, and will even allow itself to be handled, keeping the body limp. This shy, retiring snake will quickly escape if it has the opportunity, but it may also bite.

Graham Alexander

When threatened, the Rinkhals spreads a distinct hood, displaying one or two white bands in the neck region.

The Rinkhals may play dead when threatened, turning its head and part of its body upside down with its mouth agape.

Rinkhals from the KwaZulu-Natal Midlands usually have white bands both on the neck and along the body.

Unlike the Mozambique Spitting Cobra, that can spit without lifting its head, the Rinkhals only spits while spreading a hood. The raised portion of the body is thrown forward when spitting.

Coral Shield Cobras

The Coral Shield Cobra has a medium-sized shield on the nose that is clearly visible.

These smallish attractive snakes, averaging 300–600 mm in length, occur throughout most of the Cape and northwards into Namibia. They have an enlarged scale or shield on the nose that is clearly visible, hence the common name. They are very secretive and spend much of their time underground and in rock crevices, emerging at dusk to hunt for food. Coral shield cobras are particularly active after rains, with many individuals being killed by vehicles while crossing roads. They are bad-tempered snakes, but will always rather escape from, than confront, danger. If cornered, however, they will lift the head off the ground and spread a narrow hood while hissing and striking repeatedly. Very little is known about their venom, but it is thought to be dangerously neurotoxic and potentially fatal to humans.

The **Coral Shield Cobra** is orange-yellow to coral above with 20–47 narrow, black crossbars on the body and tail. It occurs from the southern Cape northwards into the southern half of Namibia, and inhabits rocky outcrops and dry, stony regions. Individuals have

The Coral Shield Cobra is a bad-tempered snake.

The Namibian Shield Cobra has dark markings on the throat. These may consist of clear dark bands or dark blotches.

When cornered and threatened, the Namibian Shield Cobra spreads a narrow hood.

Warren Schmidt

Warren Schmidt

been observed using their heads to excavate sand from beneath rocks to find suitable shelter. The snake will push its head under a rock and twist it sideways before retracting it, removing some sand in the process. The head will then be pushed back under the rock and twisted in the opposite direction. Its diet consists of lizards, rodents and small snakes. Females lay up to 11 eggs in summer.

The **Namibian Shield Cobra** grows larger than the Coral Shield Cobra. It has 24–66 black crossbars on the back that may fade completely with age. This snake inhabits karoo scrub from southern Namibia into Angola. It feeds on lizards, rodents and small snakes. The female lays up to 11 eggs in summer. The Namibian Shield Cobra appears to have more toxic venom than the Coral Shield Cobra and is known to have been responsible for the death of at least two children. These cobras are popular in private collections and are often illegally exported to the pet trade in Europe.

Coral Shield Cobras feed on lizards and rodents, but are also known to eat other snakes.

Coral Shield Cobras spread a narrow hood, but they are not able to spit their venom.

The Coral Shield Cobra is orange-yellow to coral with 20–47 narrow, black crossbars on the body and tail.

Tell-tale signs

- Enlarged scale on the nose
- Orange-yellow to coral-red with black crossbars on the body and tail
- Active at night
- Will lift the head off the ground, hiss loudly and strike repeatedly
- Form a narrow hood

Shield Cobras

Shield cobras average 450 mm, with a maximum length of 750 mm. They are grey-brown to salmon-pink or reddish-brown above with darker blotches over the body and tail. The head and neck are much darker, even black in some forms. The most obvious feature is the large scale or shield on the nose, which is used as a bulldozer when pushing through soil. These snakes hide down animal burrows or under rocks during the day and actively hunt for food at night. When cornered, shield snakes raise their bodies off the ground and hiss, like the coral shield snakes, but do not form a hood. The big scale on the nose is clearly visible when they display in this manner. They feed on small rodents, lizards, frogs and other snakes. Females produce up to 14 eggs in summer and may coil around the eggs to provide some protection. The venom is usually fairly mild, although a bite from one of these snakes may be very painful. At least one human death has been

▲ The Kalahari Shield Cobra spends most of the day in hiding, emerging at night to hunt for food.

The Kalahari Shield Cobra has a large shield on the nose, which is used to push through sand when seeking prey. ▶

Warren Schmidt

Marius Burger

▲ The Lowveld Shield Cobra lifts its head off the ground when threatened, but lacks the impressive hood shown by the larger cobras.

reported and these snakes should therefore be considered dangerous to humans.

The **Kalahari Shield Cobra** has a black head and neck, and a grey-brown to salmon pink body with darker blotches on the back. It has an extensive distribution, from central and northern Namibia through Botswana into western Zimbabwe and the North West, Mpumalanga and Limpopo provinces. Like the Rinkhals, this snake may also play dead.

The **Lowveld Shield Cobra** is very similar to the Kalahari Shield Cobra in both behaviour and coloration. It occurs in the eastern regions of Limpopo province and in most of Mpumalanga.

The **Eastern Shield Cobra** is much larger than the other two and has distinct black blotches on the back and sides. It is found in moist savanna and lowland forest in Mozambique and Zimbabwe.

▲
The Lowveld Shield Cobra is relatively short and stubby, with the head barely distinct from the rest of the body.

◀ The Kalahari Shield Cobra feeds on lizards and frogs, as well as on other snakes.

Warren Schmidt

▲
Although shield cobra venom is quite mild, it is best to treat this snake with respect – the bite could be extremely painful and at least one human death has been recorded.

Tell-tale signs

- Enormous shield on the nose
- Dark markings in the neck region that are visible when the head is lifted in a defensive pose
- Active at night
- Will lift the head off the ground and hiss, but not form a hood

Boomslang

The Boomslang has the largest eyes of any African snake, making it fairly easy to identify. ▼

The **Boomslang** or Tree Snake reaches an average length of 1.3 m, with a maximum of 2 m, and is found throughout most of southern Africa, except Lesotho and the drier western areas. It is long and slender with keeled scales and enormous eyes, the largest of any African snake. The head is distinct from the rest of the body. Juveniles are greyish with bright emerald eyes, whereas adults vary: females are usually brownish with a dirty white belly; males are bright green, sometimes with black-edged scales that may give a crossbarred appearance. Yellow and black or brick-red specimens are found in some regions. This shy snake spends most of its life in trees and shrubs, where it is well camouflaged and easily able to escape. When moving on the ground, the Boomslang will often move its head from side to side while looking ahead. Most of its hunting is done in trees, where it preys on lizards, birds and their eggs, which are swallowed whole. The Boomslang is egg-laying, and the female produces up to 27 eggs, which she deposits in a hollow tree trunk or rotting log.

◀ The Boomslang varies greatly in coloration: from dull grey to brown, black with orange sides, yellowish green to green, and sometimes with clear black markings between the scales.

As the common name indicates, this snake is strictly tree-living and spends very little time on the ground. ▼

Warren Schmidt

The male Boomslang is usually green and the female is brown; hatchlings are grey.

Boomslang hatchlings always have enormous emerald eyes with a head that looks a little too big for the body.

Contrary to popular belief, the Boomslang never hangs from trees to strike at people and very seldom bites humans. Most victims are snake handlers.

Tell-tale signs

- Enormous eyes
- Strongly keeled body scales
- Mostly in trees
- May inflate the neck up to three times its normal size when annoyed

The Boomslang is easily confused with the Green Mamba and the harmless green snakes, but the enormous eyes make it easier to tell them apart.

Should a Boomslang be threatened and not be able to escape, it will inflate the neck region to some three times its normal size and draw the head back with the neck in an S-shape, exposing the vivid skin between the neck scales. Once in this position, the snake will not hesitate to strike. The short fangs are situated quite far back in the mouth, roughly under the eyes, which makes it difficult for the Boomslang to bite, compared with mambas and cobras. The venom is dangerously haemotoxic and causes massive internal bleeding. It is, however, important to bear in mind that this arboreal snake is by no means aggressive and is extremely reluctant to bite. Very few bites are reported, and the majority of victims are snake handlers. It is a popular fallacy that the Boomslang awaits people passing under trees and then drops onto a victim.

Warren Schmidt

A well-camouflaged male Boomslang sits motionless in a tree, where it will not be easy to spot.

A female Boomslang basking in the sun. The brown colouring and large eyes assist with identification.

The Boomslang has binocular vision and moves its head from side to side in a jerky fashion.

Though very placid, this snake will inflate the front part of its neck if threatened and strike out quite viciously.

Warren Schmidt

Drop for drop, the Boomslang has the most potent venom of any African snake. Fortunately, bites are infrequent.

Vine Snakes

Vine snakes, also known as bird snakes or twig snakes, are slender snakes, averaging about 1 m in length. They are grey-brown with blotches and flecks, giving the appearance of a twig or branch. The eyes are unique in that the pupil is keyhole-shaped. Like the Boomslang, these snakes are strictly arboreal, but favour low bushes and shrubs close to the ground, where they are well camouflaged. The only giveaway is the red and black tongue that may flicker slowly from time to time. Vine snakes will remain motionless in shrubs for long periods of time, scanning the ground for prey. They will approach in short spurts, darting forward to bite prey and then holding it in their jaws, giving the venom time to take effect. Their diet consists of lizards and frogs. The alternative common name 'bird snake' is not that appropriate, as birds are seldom taken. Vine snakes possess a potent haemotoxic venom that causes massive internal bleeding and is potentially fatal to humans, but they are reluctant to bite. They are also back-fanged and, like the Boomslang, do not have hollow fangs with venom passing down the centre, as is the case in cobras and mambas. The fangs have a primitive groove down the front, down which the venom

▲
Oates' Vine Snake has binocular vision and a rather peculiar keyhole-shaped eye. It is thought that this snake has better vision than most other snakes.

Warren Schmidt

▲
The Southern Vine Snake resembles a vine and is one of the best camouflaged snakes in southern Africa.

flows. It is fortunate that bites are rare, as there is no antivenom for vine snake venom. If vine snakes are threatened and cannot escape, they will inflate their neck like the Boomslang, exposing the light skin between the scales. They will then draw their head backwards and will strike out. Males are known to engage in combat, twisting around each other as they wrestle. Females lay up to 18 eggs in summer.

The **Southern Vine Snake** is one of the smaller vine snakes, reaching a maximum length of 1.5 m. It occurs from coastal KwaZulu-Natal northwards through Mpumalanga into Swaziland, Mozambique, Limpopo, the North West province, Zimbabwe and Botswana. This snake inhabits trees and shrubs in lowland forest and savanna.

Oates' Vine Snake reaches close to 1.7 m in length. It differs from the Southern Vine Snake in that the top of its head is green. This snake is found from northern Mozambique through Zimbabwe, northern Botswana and into northern Namibia.

The **Eastern Vine Snake** reaches a maximum length of 1.4 m and occurs in northern Mozambique, eastern Zimbabwe and elsewhere further north, where it inhabits trees and shrubs in lowland forest and moist savanna.

The Eastern Vine Snake is similar to the Southern Vine Snake in appearance but has more green on its head.

Like the Boomslang, the Southern Vine Snake inflates its neck when threatened and will strike with an open mouth. Fortunately, it is also extremely placid and seldom bites.

The Southern Vine Snake will often remain motionless for hours and is virtually invisible, the only giveaway being its brightly marked tongue.

Vine snakes are also commonly known as bird snakes, however, recent studies indicate that they seldom eat birds. It was thought that vine snakes use their bright red tongues to lure birds closer, but this is extremely unlikely.

Tell-tale signs

- Perfectly camouflaged like a twig or a branch
- Keyhole-shaped pupils
- Mostly in trees and shrubs quite close to the ground
- Periodically flicker a bright red tongue
- Neck is inflated like a Boomslang when annoyed

Stiletto Snakes & Natal Black Snake

The stiletto snake is unique in that it has fairly long fixed fangs that lie backwards along the upper jaw. If held behind the head, as is often done with venomous snakes, it merely has to twist the head slightly sideways to pierce with its fang. Its venom is largely cytotoxic, or cell-destroying, causing intense pain, local swelling and, in many cases, necrosis. Many snake handlers have lost fingers from stiletto snake bites. The venom is not usually considered fatal to humans. There are two lesser-known stiletto snakes within southern Africa, the Beaked Stiletto Snake and the Eastern Congo Stiletto Snake.

The **Southern Stiletto Snake**, also known as the Burrowing Asp or Side-stabbing Snake, is a small snake averaging 300–400 mm in length. It is

The Southern Stiletto Snake is one of the few snakes that cannot be handled safely – its fangs point backwards and are concealed just under the lips.

This snake spends most of its life underground, sometimes in termite mounds.

LESSER-KNOWN STILETTO SNAKE

Beaked Stiletto Snake

Warren Schmidt

Marius Burger

A Southern Stiletto Snake with a white belly from the Kalahari.

A more typical Southern Stiletto Snake with a dark belly.

purplish brown to black above and below, although some individuals have creamy white bellies. It is a fairly non-descript snake: the head is not distinct from the body and the short tail ends in a sharp spike. Many people mistake this snake for a Mole Snake or one of the other harmless snakes. It occurs from the Eastern Cape northwards into KwaZulu-Natal, Swaziland, Mpumalanga, Gauteng, Limpopo, North West, Free State, Mozambique, Zimbabwe, Botswana and Namibia. Previously also known as the Mole Viper or Burrowing Adder, the Southern Stiletto Snake spends most of its time underground and out of sight, but is usually encountered when it emerges on warm, wet evenings. It is extremely bad-tempered and should never be molested. Any attempt to catch or hold a stiletto snake invariably results in a bite; even experienced snake handlers get bitten. These snakes feed on lizards, rodents and frogs. They are egg-laying, producing up to 7 eggs in midsummer.

The **Natal Black Snake** is much larger, averaging 600–900 mm, and is a bulkier snake, with the head barely distinct from the rest of the body. It is usually black above and below but may look greyish just prior to shedding its skin. This is a coastal snake, found from East London to eastern KwaZulu-Natal, with an isolated population in the Stutterheim area in the Eastern Cape. It spends most of its life underground and may be exposed when rocks or rotting logs are moved, or during excavations. Like the Stiletto Snake, it is often found on the surface on warm, damp evenings. The Natal Black Snake is an excellent swimmer and is occasionally seen in forest streams. It feeds on frogs, rodents and lizards, and is known to include carrion in its diet. Females lay up to 10 large, soft eggs. The venom of this snake has not been studied and bites are rare. It is not thought to be potentially fatal to humans and is a docile snake that seldom attempts to bite.

The Natal Black Snake can easily be confused with some of the lesser venomous or harmless snakes.

The slow-moving, inoffensive Natal Black Snake spends most of its life underground and is seldom seen.

Warren Schmidt

Like the Southern Stiletto Snake, the Natal Black Snake may be found on the surface on a warm, damp evening, especially after rain.

Tell-tale signs

- Stout with small, blunt head and small eyes
- Tail may end in a sharp spike
- May move in jerky movements with arched neck
- May be found on the surface on warm, wet summer nights
- Live underground but may be exposed when rocks or logs are moved

Sand & Whip Snakes

▲ The Olive Whip Snake is the largest of the region's sand and whip snakes.

There are about 13 sand and whip snakes in southern Africa, varying in size from 300 mm (Dwarf Whip Snake) to over 1.8 m (Olive Whip Snake). Most of them are long and slender and, with one or two exceptions, have stripes from head to tail, either down the centre of the back or sides; otherwise they have broad bands that run from head to tail. They are extremely fast-moving and are active during the day. If disturbed, they will usually dart for cover in the closest shrub or bush, or down a hole. Upon reaching the shrub they will freeze and rely on their excellent camouflage to escape detection. If captured by the tip of the tail, these snakes may spin and snap a piece of the tail off before escaping. Many sand and whip snakes have truncated tails from previous encounters with predators. They feed largely on lizards, but will also take rodents and other snakes. These snakes are back-fanged and their venom is rather mild and is of little consequence to man.

The **Western Stripe-bellied Sand Snake** averages 1 m in length and has distinct stripes down the body, with a lemon-yellow belly. It occurs throughout much of the northern half of southern Africa, and frequents rivers, dams and cattle drinking holes in search of water. This snake is often seen during the hottest part of the day and is extremely quick to escape. It may well be one of the fastest snakes in southern Africa. Females lay up to 10 eggs in summer.

▲ Sand and whip snakes are alert snakes that hunt their prey during the day.

▲ A Western Stripe-bellied Sand Snake moves through long grass in search of lizards and rodents.

Warren Schmidt

The **Olive Whip Snake** is plain brown above, sometimes with black markings that can form lines, and has dark mottling in the vicinity of the lips. It occurs from KwaZulu-Natal northwards into Swaziland, Mpumalanga, Limpopo province, Mozambique, Zimbabwe, northern Botswana and northern Namibia. It may be mistaken for the Black Mamba as it also raises its head off the ground. Though ground-living, the Olive Whip Snake also ventures into shrubs and trees in search of food. Females lay up to 30 eggs in summer.

Like most sand and whip snakes, this Short-snouted Whip Snake has markings from head to tail.

Graham Alexander

A Short-snouted Whip Snake hatching from an egg. Most hatchlings are perfect replicas of the adults.

An unusual Crossed Whip Snake, with an orange-red tinge, and lacking the more usual stripes running from head to tail.

Tell-tale signs

- Long and slender with a fairly long head
- Medium to large eyes with round pupils
- Narrow stripes or broad bands from head to tail
- Very fast-moving and active during the day

The majority of sand and whip snakes look similar, with stripes and markings down the body, and are difficult to tell apart.

The **Short-snouted Whip Snake** averages 600 mm in length and is brown with black lines down its back. It occurs from KwaZulu-Natal through Swaziland, into Mpumalanga, Gauteng, Limpopo, North West, Zimbabwe, Botswana and central Namibia. This is a shy, nervous snake that quickly dashes for cover when disturbed and will bite readily if caught. The

Warren Schmidt

A Western Stripe-bellied Sand Snake slowly moves through shrubs in search of food. ▶

When disturbed, the Short-snouted Whip Sanke will dash off into the closest shrub, remaining motionless and relying on their camouflage to escape detection.
▼

LESSER-KNOWN SAND AND WHIP SNAKES

Niels Jacobsen   Bill Branch   Randy Babb   Wulf Haacke

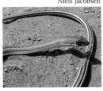

Jalla's Sand Snake   Eastern Stripe-bellied   Karoo Whip Snake   Cape Whip Snake   Kalahari Whip Snake
                        Sand Snake

venom is mild and of no consequence to humans. Females lay up to 15 eggs at a time and may produce 2 clutches in summer.

The **Crossed Whip Snake** is one of the smaller snakes in the group, averaging 600 mm in length. It frequents scrub-covered sandy areas in the Cape, but is equally at home in grasslands on top of the KwaZulu-Natal Drakensberg. Coloration is varied, with the majority having a broad dark brown stripe down the back, but unmarked brown individuals are also found. Females lay up to 13 eggs.

▲
The Crossed Whip Snake is one of the region's endemic snakes – it occurs exclusively in South Africa.

▲
The Crossed Whip Snake is commonly found in sandy, scrub-covered areas of the Cape coast.

◀ The Crossed Whip Snake, like all of the sand and whip snakes, is an egg-layer, producing 3–13 eggs in summer.

The Crossed Whip Snake is the smallest of the whip snakes, averaging 600 mm in length.
▼

Richard Boycott

Wulf Haacke

Namib Whip Snake

Dwarf Whip Snake

Leopard Whip Snake

Western Whip Snake

Skaapstekers

A Spotted Skaapsteker from Gauteng.

Skaapstekers are very similar to sand and whip snakes in behaviour. They can be found in a variety of habitats, from fynbos at sea level to savanna on mountain tops. They are alert and fast-moving, and hunt for food during the day. The common name 'skaapsteker' means 'sheep stabber' and these snakes are often incorrectly held responsible for sheep deaths. They are back-fanged and have a mild venom that cannot kill sheep. The venom is of no danger to humans.

The **Spotted** or **Rhombic Skaapsteker** averages around 500 mm in length and has either stripes or dark-edged mottles down the back. Specimens from the Western Cape and the KwaZulu-Natal Drakensberg differ markedly in coloration. The Spotted Skaapsteker occurs from the Western Cape, through KwaZulu-Natal to the Free State, Gauteng and has populations in Namaqualand and parts of Namibia. This snake is quick to dash off and

A Spotted Skaapsteker from Lambert's Bay on the West Coast.

Despite its reputation, the Spotted Skaapsteker has mild venom that is of no danger to humans.

LESSER-KNOWN SKAAPSTEKER

Grey-bellied Grass Snake

A Spotted Skaapsteker from the KwaZulu-Natal Drakensberg.

hide in a shrub, or it will coil around a grass tuft where it is well camouflaged. It is also reputed to play dead like the Rinkhals. The Spotted Skaapsteker actively hunts for its food and preys on lizards, rodents, birds and frogs. Snakes are also eaten. Females lay up to 30 eggs.

The **Striped Skaapsteker** averages around 600 mm in length and has several dark and light bands and stripes down the body. It prefers arid regions, from the Free State to Gauteng, Limpopo, and North West, into Zimbabwe, Botswana and northern Namibia. This snake favours open grassland and vlei areas and, despite the vivid markings, is well camouflaged. Females lay up to 18 eggs in summer and do not coil around their eggs like the Spotted Skaapsteker. Although venomous, it poses no threat to humans. Like most of the sand and whip snakes, this snake will twist vigorously if held by the tail, snapping off the tip to escape.

Warren Schmidt

Although the Striped Skaapsteker has vivid markings, it is well camouflaged in grass and is difficult to see.

The Striped Skaapsteker will often hide among rocks and building rubble close to homes.

Spotted Skaapsteker females lay eggs under rocks or in other sheltered spots and will coil around the eggs to protect them. The embryos are already partially developed when the eggs are laid, reducing the incubation period to around 6 weeks. The hatchlings measure 150–240 mm in length. The python is another snake species that coils around its eggs.

Tell-tale signs

- Large eyes with round pupils
- Very well camouflaged among grass and shrubs
- Active during the day
- Nervous and fast-moving, dashing for cover when disturbed

Tiger Snakes

The slow-moving Common Tiger Snake is active at night, when it will also climb into trees in search of food.

There are two species of tiger snake in southern Africa. These snakes are orange-pink above with dark brown blotches down the back and onto the tail. The broad head is distinct from the neck, and the eye is large with a vertical pupil. These snakes are back-fanged and are mildly venomous.

The **Common Tiger Snake** averages around 800 mm in length and has 22–75 dark blackish blotches down the back and tail. This snake occurs from KwaZulu-Natal through Swaziland, Mozambique, Mpumalanga, Limpopo, North West, Free State, and into Botswana and Namibia. It is active at night and will hide in rock crevices or under the bark of trees during the day. It is slow-moving, and is equally at home on the ground and in trees. Individuals are occasionally found in the rafters of thatched roofs. It feeds on lizards but is known to take fledgling birds and bats. Females lay up to 20 eggs in summer. If cornered, it will draw its head back in an S-shape, flattened horizontally, and strike quite viciously. It is mildly venomous, however, and poses no threat to humans.

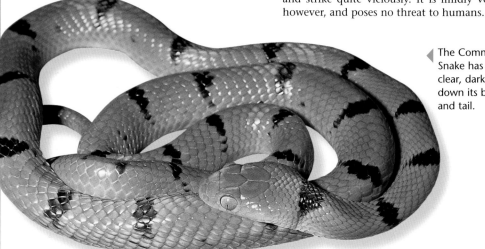

The Common Tiger Snake has 22–75 clear, dark crossbars down its back and tail.

This snake has a split pupil – a characteristic of many of the nocturnal snakes.

When threatened, the tiger snake draws its head back into a striking position, often with the tongue flickering.

Warren Schmidt

Graham Alexander

Beetz's Tiger Snake is restricted to the drier west and is quite similar to the Common Tiger Snake in appearance and size. It has 42–59 dark blotches on the back and tail. This snake occurs from the southern Cape to Free State, Namaqualand and southern Namibia, but is absent from the desert. It is a rock-living snake and spends the day hiding in narrow rock crevices. Hunting is done at night, and many of these snakes are killed by vehicles when crossing roads, especially in parts of Namaqualand where roads transect rocky habitat. Its diet consists of lizards, especially geckos. Females lay up to 5 elongate eggs in summer.

Beetz's Tiger Snake usually has a much larger dark blotch on the neck than the Common Tiger Snake.

Warren Schmidt

Graham Alexander

Beetz's Tiger Snake has 42–59 dark blotches on the back and tail.

Beetz's Tiger Snake is found in the western half of southern Africa, where it inhabits rocky ridges in the Karoo.

Tell-tale signs

- Eyes are large with vertical pupils
- Several dark crossbars across the back and tail
- Active at night and often seen on roads, especially after summer rains
- May draw the head back when threatened and strike viciously

Herald Snake

The Herald Snake shows white speckles.

The **Herald** or **Red-lipped Snake** averages around 500 mm in length. It is a grey to olive-green snake with scattered white speckles, a white underside, and a dark head that is distinct from the rest of the body. The lips are either white or orange to bright red, hence the common name. This snake has a wide distribution, extending northwards from the southwestern Cape through the Eastern Cape, Free State, KwaZulu-Natal, Mpumalanga, Swaziland, Gauteng, Limpopo, and North West, into Mozambique, Zimbabwe and northern Botswana. During the day it hides in rockeries, in compost heaps and under building rubble. Because of its unique coloration, it cannot easily be confused with any other snake. The Herald Snake is sometimes incorrectly referred to as a night adder, as it

Warren Schmidt

Because it is active at night, the Herald Snake is sometimes incorrectly called a night adder.

When threatened, the Herald Snake draws its head back in a striking position and flattens it horizontally, exposing the upper lips that may be brightly coloured.

is often seen at night in suburban gardens. It prefers damp locations, especially gardens with fish ponds, which attract frogs and toads. As its venom is rather ineffective at subduing toads, it tends to hang on to its prey for long periods before swallowing. Females lay up to 19 eggs in early summer. The newly hatched young are minute, sometimes only 80 mm in length. When threatened, the Herald Snake puts up an impressive display. It will draw the head back in an S-shape, lift it off the ground and flatten it horizontally, showing the upper lips, which may be bright red. This snake will strike viciously and repeatedly but is back-fanged with a rather mild venom. The venom is of no consequence to humans and takes a long time to kill even a toad. The Herald Snake does bite readily, however.

The Herald Snake usually has a dark head that is distinct from the rest of the body. It defends itself by striking viciously and repeatedly – although its venom is mild and presents no danger to humans.

Some individuals have bright red or orange lips, hence the common name 'Red-lipped Snake'.

Warren Schmidt

The common name Herald Snake comes from the newspaper *The Eastern Province Herald* in the Eastern Cape, which first announced the presence of this snake. It is also known as the Red-lipped Snake, because of the colour of the upper lip in some individuals.

Tell-tale signs

- Some specimens have orange to bright red upper lips
- Grey body with white speckling and darker head
- Active at night and may frequent suburban gardens in search of toads
- Prefer damp localities
- May draw the head back when threatened and strike viciously

Purple-glossed Snakes

A Natal Purple-glossed Snake.

The purple-glossed snakes look quite similar and can be difficult to tell apart. This individual is a Natal Purple-glossed Snake.

There are 5 species of purple-glossed snake, all very similar to the Natal Black Snake and difficult to distinguish from it. They are thick-bodied snakes with blunt heads barely distinct from the rest of the body. Coloration is uniform glossy dark brown to black with a purplish sheen. They may look dull grey in colour just before shedding. These are burrowing snakes that are seldom encountered as most of their lives are spent underground. They are back-fanged and venomous, but their venom is not considered dangerous to man.

The **Natal Purple-glossed Snake** averages 500 mm in length and is found from the KwaZulu-Natal lowlands to Swaziland, Mpumalanga, Gauteng and Limpopo Province. It is a burrowing snake that prefers humic soil and wooded or forest habitats, where it is rare and seldom encountered. It may be found on the surface on hot, wet evenings and is reluctant to bite. It preys on lizards and other snakes. It appears as though this snake lays eggs and gives birth to live young. Up to 11 eggs have been found, and a female in Gauteng produced 12 live young.

A Common Purple-glossed Snake.

The venom of this snake has not been studied.

Bryan Maritz

The **Common Purple-glossed Snake** grows larger, averaging 750 mm, but can reach a length of 1.12 m. This snake occurs from KwaZulu-Natal through Swaziland, Mpumalanga, Limpopo and into Mozambique, Zimbabwe and Botswana. It is a secretive snake that is seldom seen. Individuals are forced to the surface when the ground becomes waterlogged, otherwise it is found under rocks and logs. When threatened, it may hide its head under some body coils and move the tip of its tail to distract its aggressor. This snake feeds on burrowing reptiles such as blind snakes, legless lizards and amphisbaenids. The purple-glossed snakes have not been studied well, and the reproduction of the Common Purple-glossed Snake is still uncertain. It is thought that it lays eggs, but the number of eggs produced is not known.

Purple-glossed snakes feed on burrowing reptiles like blind snakes and legless lizards.

Graham Alexander

A Common Purple-glossed Snake.

Purple-glossed snakes spend most of their life underground and are not frequently seen.

Tell-tale signs

- Thick-bodied, with blunt head and small eyes
- Body may have a purplish sheen
- Live underground but may be exposed when rocks or logs are moved
- May be found on the surface on warm, wet summer nights

Pythons

The Southern African Python is the region's longest snake, reaching a length of nearly 6 m.

Though not venomous, this snake has strong recurved teeth and can inflict a rather nasty bite.

Pythons are often referred to as giant snakes, and are the African and Asian versions of the boas and anacondas of the Americas. They are primitive snakes, and still retain the vestiges of hind limbs in the form of a nail that is visible on either side of the snake's anal region. This nail serves little purpose as far as we know, but may be used during mating to stimulate the female – males have much larger nails than females. Heat-sensitive pits on the lips serve as infrared 'eyes' and enable the snakes to detect minute fluctuations in temperature. These heat sensory pits function at night when they hunt warm-blooded prey. Several other snakes, such as the boas, anacondas, rattlesnakes and pit vipers, have similar heat-sensory pits.

The **Southern African Python** is by far the largest and bulkiest snake in Africa, reaching a length of around 6 m and a weight of more than 50 kg. The head is distinct from the body, which is covered in light and dark speckling and blotches, providing excellent camouflage. Old individuals are often very dark in colour. The Southern African Python is found from the Eastern Cape, northwards into KwaZulu-Natal, Swaziland, Mozambique, Mpumalanga, Gauteng, Limpopo, North West, Zimbabwe, Botswana and Namibia. Large pythons often live down aardvark holes and will bask near the hole during the day. At night they either hunt for food or await prey in ambush. They are known for their ability to kill and eat large animals such as antelope, and it is often incorrectly thought that

Southern African Pythons are able to take down large prey such as Impala.

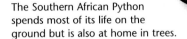

they crush their prey to death. Once captured, the prey is quickly constricted, and pressure on the heart and circulatory system causes death, not crushing or prolonged suffocation. It is also a popular fallacy that a python needs to hook its tail around a tree before it can attack a large animal or human. Like most other snakes, pythons are at home in water and can swim well. Females produce 30–60, but as many as 100 eggs, each a little smaller than a tennis ball. Though not venomous, pythons have many strongly recurved teeth and are capable of inflicting painful bites. They bite readily and may lunge repeatedly – a bite will cause extensive tissue damage and may require stitches. Although these snakes have killed people in the past, there are very few large individuals left. Stories of python attacks are usually fabricated by people who have killed a python and either fear retribution or wish to sell the meat, skin and fat to the 'muti' trade.

Anchieta's Dwarf Python is not a giant snake, averaging just over 1 m, with a maximum length just short of 2 m. It is reddish-brown in colour with darker and lighter blotches and a light, spotted belly. This snake is found from central Namibia northwards into Angola. It is rare and is sought-after in the international pet trade – smuggled individuals will sell for tens of thousands of Rands. Anchieta's Dwarf Python is found in riverine bush or dry, rocky sandveld regions and is primarily active at night. If confronted, it may roll up into a defensive ball, like the Royal Python of West Africa. Like the Southern African Python, it prefers warm-blooded prey and feeds on rodents and birds. Females produce up to 5 eggs in summer.

The Southern African Python spends most of its life on the ground but is also at home in trees.

Southern African Pythons lay up to 100 eggs, usually in an aardvark or other hole large enough to accommodate the female. Once the eggs have been laid, the female will coil around them to protect them and assist with incubation. The female basks at the burrow entrance to absorb heat and increase her body temperature. Her body temperature may reach in excess of 40 °C, close to a lethal temperature for snakes. Once warmed up, she returns to the burrow and coils around her eggs to increase the incubation temperature. The young remain with the mother for about one month after hatching.

Warren Schmidt

Anchieta's Dwarf Python, also known simply as the Dwarf Python, seldom exceeds 1.8 m in length.

Tell-tale signs

- Robust, bulky snakes with the head clearly distinct from the body
- Heat-sensory pits on the lips are clearly visible as holes on the upper lip
- Mainly found on the ground, but may climb into trees and shrubs
- Active at dusk or at night but fond of basking in the sun

Pythons, like rattlesnakes and pit vipers, have heat sensory pits on the upper lip.

House & Rock Snakes

Juvenile snakes are often more brightly coloured than the adults.

House and rock snakes are largely active at night. They are slow-moving snakes, non-venomous and of no danger to man. They include rodents and other small mammals, lizards and sometimes frogs in their diet.

The harmless **Brown House Snake** is very common, and adults average around 600–900 mm in length. They vary in colour from uniform light brown to reddish-brown or dark brown above, with a mother-of-pearl belly. They are easy to identify – there is a light stripe on either side of the head running from the tip of the snout through the eye to the back of the head, and another light stripe from the eye to the angle of the jaw. The upper light stripe may extend down the sides of the body. This snake seeks shelter under building rubble or under corrugated asbestos sheets, where it hunts rodents. It is very effective at controlling them and often devours an entire rodent family in one sitting. This is a popular snake among young collectors as it settles down well, feeds easily and lives for as long as 10 years. It is found throughout most of southern Africa. It has adapted well to suburbia and is frequently found near houses, hence the common name. Between 8 and 18 eggs are produced in summer, with the young measuring 190–260 mm.

Brown House Snakes from Namaqualand often have bulging eyes.

A pinkish Brown House Snake from Namaqualand.

A Brown House Snake from Springbok, Namaqualand.

A light Brown House Snake from Aus, Namibia.

A typical Brown House Snake from KwaZulu-Natal.

The **Olive House Snake** is not very common and is much smaller than the Brown House Snake, averaging 450–750 mm in length. It is uniform olive-green to olive-grey or blackish above, with a similar coloured belly. This elusive snake is endemic to South Africa and is found in parts of the Western and Eastern Cape, KwaZulu-Natal, Mpumalanga, Limpopo and parts of Gauteng. Females lay 5–15 eggs in summer, the hatchlings measuring 190–240 mm in length. The Olive House Snake has a preference for moist habitats. Like the other house snakes, it is completely harmless.

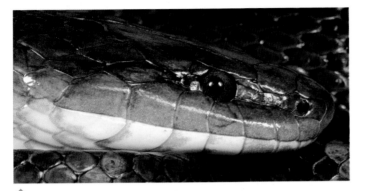

The Olive House Snake prefers damp localities and is not often seen.

A light-coloured Olive House Snake from Limpopo.

The Olive House Snake, like the other house snakes, is completely harmless and poses no threat to humans.

A dark-coloured Olive House Snake from KwaZulu-Natal.

Tell-tale signs

- Slow-moving
- Reluctant to bite
- May be encountered in residential gardens
- Largely ground-living and active at night
- Feed largely on rodents and lizards

Warren Schmidt

The **Aurora House Snake** is similar in length to the Olive House Snake, reaching a maximum length of 900 mm. It is olive-green above with a bright yellow to orange, narrow stripe down the centre of the head and back, and a light, greenish-white belly. This is another southern African endemic, and is found in the Western and Eastern Cape, northwards into KwaZulu-Natal, Lesotho, Free State, Gauteng, parts of Mpumalanga, Limpopo and the North West province. Much of its habitat appears to have been destroyed by development, and it is becoming quite rare. Although largely active at night, it may bask in the early mornings or late afternoons and is active on overcast days. Between 8 and 12 eggs are produced in summer, the young measuring 200–225 mm. This snake is harmless.

The Aurora House Snake has become quite rare, as much of its habitat has been destroyed by urban development.

Warren Schmidt

The Aurora House Snake is a harmless snake that relies on its muscle power to subdue its prey. House snakes are not venomous.

The Aurora House Snake has a clear orange to yellow stripe running from its head, down its body and onto its tail.

LESSER-KNOWN HOUSE AND ROCK SNAKES

Warren Schmidt

Swazi Rock Snake

Yellow-bellied House Snake

Fisk's House Snake

The **Spotted Rock Snake** has an average length of 300–500 mm. Coloration varies somewhat, from brown to pinkish-grey above with darker spots and blotches on the back that may form a zigzag pattern. The belly is white to yellowish-white. It has a wide distribution and is found from southern Namibia into Namaqualand, the Northern and Eastern Cape, KwaZulu-Natal, Mpumalanga, Lesotho, Swaziland, Limpopo and parts of Gauteng. This is a rock-living snake that hides in narrow rock crevices, emerging at night to hunt for geckos and other lizards. Between 3 and 6 eggs are laid in summer. Like the other snakes in the group, the Spotted Rock Snake is completely harmless.

▲
A Spotted Rock Snake from KwaZulu-Natal.

▲
A Spotted Rock Snake from Namaqualand.

Warren Schmidt

▲
The Spotted Rock Snake is a specialist that lives in narrow rock cracks and feeds largely on geckos.

The Spotted Rock Snake has dark pairs of blotches down its back that sometimes join. It is not easily confused with any other snake. ▶

Water Snakes

There are 4 species of water snake in southern Africa. These snakes are medium-sized and spend most of their lives in or very close to water. They are cylindrical, with fairly large eyes and are mostly quite dull and nondescript in colour. These snakes are largely active at night, though some move about during the day in well-shaded streams. Water snakes feed largely on amphibians and fish. The much-feared *Ivuzamanzi* is a water snake and, like all of these snakes, has no venom and is harmless.

The **Common Brown Water Snake** averages 500 mm in length and is a slender, light brown to dark brown snake with a salmon-pink belly. It occurs from the Western Cape through the Eastern Cape into KwaZulu-Natal, Lesotho, Free State, Gauteng, Mpumalanga, Swaziland, Limpopo, North West and into Zimbabwe. This snake is an excellent swimmer and is usually found in damp localities near vleis, rivers and streams, where it hunts mainly at night. It is a common snake that may often be encountered when it crosses roads. This powerful constrictor feeds on frogs and fish, and occasionally on rodents and birds. It is an egg-laying snake, with females producing up to 23 eggs in midsummer.

▲
The Common Brown Water Snake feeds on frogs and tadpoles, as well as fish.

Graham Alexander

▲
The Common Brown Water Snake is active at night and frequents damp localities, where it actively hunts its prey.

The **Dusky-bellied Water Snake** is a bigger snake, averaging 800 mm, but reaching a maximum length of 1.2 m. It is brownish-black to black above, with a creamy yellow belly that has dark blotches forming a band down the centre, hence the common name. The Dusky-bellied Water Snake occurs from the Eastern Cape into KwaZulu-Natal, Mpumalanga and Swaziland. It is far more aquatic than the Common Brown Water Snake and favours well-shaded streams and rivers, where it can be seen hunting for food during the day. It will often swim totally submerged, searching for frogs and fish. Smaller prey is easily swallowed underwater, but larger prey may be constricted and carried to the water's edge to swallow. Females produce up to 17 eggs. Unlike the Common Brown Water Snake, which is very placid, this snake often appears to be bad-tempered and bites repeatedly when handled. It is not venomous and poses no threat to humans.

The Dusky-bellied Water Snake has a cream to orange-yellow belly with darker markings or blotches, hence the common name.

Like the Common Brown Water Snake, the Dusky-bellied Water Snake also feeds on frogs and fish and may swallow its prey underwater.

The Dusky-bellied Water Snake lives near shaded streams, where it spends a great deal of its time in water.

Tell-tale signs

- May have dark markings down the centre of the belly
- Hunt in shaded streams during the day or night
- Largely active at night and on overcast days
- Aquatic, but equally at home on land
- Able to feed underwater, but tend to take large prey to land before swallowing

Mole Snake

Juvenile Mole Snakes are brightly coloured with dark blotches, light spots and mottling.

The **Mole Snake** is a large, robust snake that averages just over 1 m, but has been known to exceed 2 m in length. It has a stout body with a small head and pointed snout. Juveniles are brightly coloured with mottles or zigzag markings, while most adults are plain, light brown to dark brown or black, sometimes with mottling. This large and powerful snake moves about during the day, pushing its way through soft sand and mole burrows in search of food. It feeds on a variety of rodents and will usually seize its prey by the head and constrict it before swallowing it. Birds and their eggs are also eaten, and the eggs are swallowed whole. Juvenile Mole Snakes also feed on lizards. Males are known to engage in combat.

A plain olive-brown Mole Snake showing its characteristic pointed snout.

As they grow, juvenile Mole Snakes lose their bright colours, becoming uniformly brown.

This dark brown Mole Snake shows scars from battles with rival males.

This is one of few species where the males bite each other, leaving gaping holes. One snake will latch onto another and move the head up and down, similar to the action of a tin opener, often cutting deep enough to expose ribs. These wounds heal quickly, leaving ugly scars. Mole Snakes are often bad-tempered and will strike repeatedly with the mouth agape. They are found throughout most of southern Africa, but are not as common as people think: other snakes are often wrongly identified as Mole Snakes. Females produce around 30, but as many as 95, live young at a time during late summer. Unfortunately, the non-venomous Mole Snake is often mistaken for a dangerous Cape Cobra and killed. Though it possesses no venom, it does have very sharp teeth and a bite will often result in the victim requiring medical assistance and stitches.

Though not venomous, the Mole Snake is capable of inflicting a nasty bite with its powerful teeth.

When cornered, a Mole Snake will draw its head back into a striking position. They bite readily.

As the common name indicates, the Mole Snake goes down mole burrows in search of food. It also feeds on other rodents, lizards, birds and their eggs.

Tell-tale signs

- The head is small and pointed
- Large and robust body, may exceed 2 m in length
- Spends much of its time in mammal burrows but is active during the day

Green Snakes

▲ A Spotted Bush Snake.

Green snakes are thin, alert snakes that are only active during the day. At night they sleep in narrow crevices, often in tree trunks, or high up on the outer branches of trees, shrubs and hedges. It is easy for them to drop to the ground and escape if a predator approaches while they are sleeping. These snakes are excellent climbers and have keeled scales on their bellies to aid climbing up the rough bark of trees or other uneven surfaces, like face-brick walls. This often results in their ending up in houses or outbuildings, where they shelter from the heat or hunt for food. They prey on little frogs, such as reed frogs, and geckos, especially Tropical House Geckos, which have become extremely common on the walls of houses and which feed on insects attracted to the exterior lights. These snakes are completely harmless and are quick to escape into the closest push or shrub when disturbed.

The **Spotted Bush Snake** has an average length of 600–900 mm and is fairly thin. Coloration is usually bright green above with black spots or crossbars that fade about halfway down the back. The belly is whitish to yellowish. This snake has a wide distribution throughout the eastern half of southern Africa, from the Eastern Cape through KwaZulu-Natal, Mozambique, Swaziland, Mpumalanga, Gauteng, Limpopo, Zimbabwe and much of Botswana, with a population occurring from northern Namibia into Namaqualand. The Spotted Bush Snake is frequently seen in bushes and shrubs in suburban gardens, but is quick to escape. While seeking prey it may sway its head from side to side as though it is trying to get a better view. This snake is completely harmless.

▲ A Western Green Snake swallows a sizeable gecko.

LESSER-KNOWN GREEN SNAKE

Angola Green Snake

▲ The Spotted Green Snake is bright green above with black spots or crossbars that fade towards the tail.

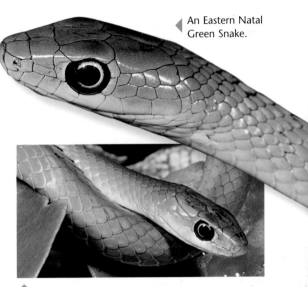

An Eastern Natal Green Snake.

The **Western** and **Eastern Natal Green Snakes** average 750–900 mm in length. They are also bright green, but lack the Spotted Bush Snake's black marking or crossbars. These snakes occur from the Eastern Cape through KwaZulu-Natal into Swaziland, Mozambique, Mpumalanga and Gauteng. They are often confused with the Green Mamba, but are much thinner and have golden-orange eyes. Their diet consists of lizards, especially geckos, and frogs, but not toads. Between 4 and 14 eggs are produced in summer, with the young measuring 150 mm in length. These harmless snakes are alert and are excellent climbers.

The **Green Water Snake** is the smaller of the green snakes, averaging 600 mm. It is bright emerald-green above with a white belly. Some individuals to the north may have a few dark bars above in the neck region. This snake is found from the Eastern Cape through KwaZulu-Natal, Mozambique, Mpumalanga and the eastern parts of Gauteng, into Zimbabwe and further north. It spends most of its time on the ground in moist areas. When disturbed, it is very quick to escape. It is a harmless snake, and preys on frogs, often catching them in water. Between 3 and 8 elongate eggs are laid in summer, with the young measuring 150–200 mm.

A Western Natal Green Snake.

Green snakes are active and alert snakes that hunt in daylight.

Warren Schmidt

A Green Water Snake.

Any green snake that is thinner than a human's smallest finger is perfectly harmless, **with one exception**. The Green Mamba is about 300–450 mm when it hatches and about as thick as a small finger. It is confined to coastal bush from the Eastern Cape through KwaZulu-Natal, into Mozambique and eastern Zimbabwe. It does not have a white or yellowish belly. Larger Green Mambas (>600 mm) are as thick as an adult's index finger or thicker.

Tell-tale signs

- Large eyes with orange to golden or yellow round pupils
- Long, slender, green and seldom thicker than a person's finger
- Some may have black markings
- Active during the day
- Equally at home on the ground and in trees
- Some are excellent climbers and can scale face-brick walls
- Good swimmers, but usually swim on the surface

Most of the green snakes have golden-yellow pupils.

Slug-eaters

▲
An unmarked Common Slug-eater.

Slug-eaters feed on snails and slugs, and prefer damp localities.
▼

There are 2 species of slug-eater in southern Africa. These stout, slow-moving snakes have small heads that are barely distinct from the rest of the body, and small eyes. Slug-eaters are specialist feeders, targeting slugs and snails. They follow slug and snail slime trails and devour their prey with much slime and foam bulging from the mouth. When eating a snail, the snake will bite onto the forepart of its prey and slowly pull it from its shell.

The **Common Slug-eater** averages 300 mm, with a maximum length of just over 400 mm. It is greyish, with a broad reddish band running along the centre of the back. This snake is found from the Western Cape northwards into the Free State, Lesotho, KwaZulu-Natal, Swaziland, Mpumalanga, Gauteng, Limpopo and Zimbabwe. It is very common in some areas, including suburban gardens, and is completely harmless. This useful snake targets slugs and snails, which do a great deal of damage to gardens. It moves about slowly during the day and can be found under any form of shelter such as rocks, logs or even grass tufts. Females produce up to 22 live young. It is reluctant to bite when handled, but may make use of its powerful scent glands to repel attackers. Otherwise it rolls into a tight spiral with the head concealed, hence the Afrikaans name 'tabakrolletjie'.

◄ The Common Slug-eater produces up to 22 live young at a time.

A typically coloured Common Slug-eater with a broad band down its back.
▼

Warren Schmidt

The **Variegated Slug-eater** is similar in size to the Common Slug-eater but the large females appear to be bulkier. These snakes may have dark spots or blotches down the back, but the markings may fade with age. It occurs in coastal forest from northern Zululand into southern Mozambique. This is a secretive, slow-moving snake that hunts during the day and night, but tends to remain under leaf litter, decaying vegetation or even loose sand. Up to 20 young are born in summer. This snake has not been observed rolling up in a tight spiral like the Common Slug-eater. It is reluctant to bite.

Slug-eaters are completely harmless to humans.

The Variegated Slug-eater usually has dark spots or blotches down its back.

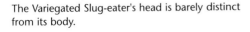

The Variegated Slug-eater's head is barely distinct from its body.

Tell-tale signs

- Head small and barely distinct from the body
- Powerful glands in the tail region may emit a foul-smelling substance if handled
- Favour damp localities where snails and slugs are abundant

Wolf Snakes

Wolf snakes have wolf-like teeth, from which they get their name.

The Common Wolf Snake has a flattened head with small eyes and vertical pupils.

Wolf snakes are small snakes with flattened heads that are barely distinct from the rest of the body, and small eyes with vertical pupils. They are active at night and have large recurved teeth in the front of the mouth, hence the common name 'wolf snake'.

The **Common Wolf Snake** averages 350 mm in length and is light brown to purplish-brown or black above, sometimes with white-edged scales that give a speckled effect. This snake occurs from the Eastern Cape northwards into Lesotho, Free State, KwaZulu-Natal, Gauteng, the Northern Cape, North West, Limpopo, Mozambique, Zimbabwe, Botswana and Namibia. It is a ground-living snake that inhabits a variety of habitats from lowland forest to moist savanna and karoo scrub. It hunts at night and is slow-moving, looking for lizards, especially skinks. The teeth are an adaptation for catching smooth-bodied skinks. In suburban areas it is often found hiding in rubbish heaps or under thatch grass, while elsewhere it lives in deserted termite mounds or under rocks. Females lay up to 9 eggs in early summer. When threatened, it may flatten its entire body but is reluctant to bite. Wolf snakes are completely harmless. Snake enthusiasts should be cautious, as it is easy to mistake a wolf snake for a stiletto snake.

The harmless Common Wolf Snake is easily confused with a variety of other snakes, including venomous ones such as the Southern Stiletto Snake.

The **Variegated Wolf Snake** has an average length of 300–360 mm. As the common name suggests, this snake is black with white markings. It favours rocky habitat as well as dead aloes, and occurs in northern Zululand to Swaziland, Mpumalanga, Limpopo and Zimbabwe. Females lay up to 3 eggs.

The **Pygmy Wolf Snake** is one of the smallest of the wolf snakes, averaging 150–180 mm. It occurs in lowland forest in northern Zululand where it shelters under logs and grass tussocks. This snake has also been found in exotic pine plantations. If feeds exclusively on burrowing legless skinks. Females lay up to 3 eggs.

Niels Jacobsen

A Variegated Wolf Snake.

The Pygmy Wolf Snake is one of the smallest wolf snakes and occurs in northern Zululand.

The Pygmy Wolf Snake has a white band around the snout.

Tell-tale signs

- Small, flattened head, barely distinct from the body
- Small, slender body
- Seen on the ground
- Active at night
- Easily confused with the venomous stiletto snakes

File Snakes

▲
The Southern File Snake has a triangular body with very distinct raised scales, hence the common name.

There are 3 species of file snake in southern Africa. These unusual snakes have triangular bodies and strongly keeled scales, hence the common name. The head is broad and flat and is distinct from the rest of the body. File snakes are active at night and are slow-moving. They are secretive snakes and are not encountered very often.

The **Southern File Snake**, formerly known as the Cape File Snake, reaches an average length of 1 m, with a maximum of almost 2 m. It is grey-brown to purplish-brown above with a distinct white stripe down the centre of the back extending from the neck to the tail. It resembles a file due to the strongly keeled scales on the back. The Southern File Snake occurs from the Eastern Cape, through KwaZulu-Natal into Swaziland, Mozambique, Mpumalanga, Limpopo, North West, Botswana and northern Namibia. During the day it hides in hollow logs or holes in the ground; at night it hunts for food, often venturing into shrubs and bushes. Individuals are sometimes encountered

▲
File snakes are not venomous and feed on reptiles, including other snakes like mambas and Puff Adders.

at night after summer rains. They feed mainly on snakes, including venomous snakes such as mambas and Puff Adders, and appear to be immune to the venom of these species. The prey is seized and often swallowed while still alive. Females lay up to 13 eggs and may produce more than one clutch per season. It is a docile, inoffensive and completely harmless snake. Although reluctant to bite, it emits a foul-smelling substance from glands in the tail region when handled. These snakes are highly prized in snake collections, and there is a lot of illegal dealing in file snakes.

The **Black File Snake** is much smaller, averaging 450 mm, and is uniform purple-brown to black in colour. This snake occurs from northern KwaZulu-Natal around Durban to Swaziland, Mpumalanga, Limpopo, Zimbabwe, Botswana and Namibia. This snake is strictly ground-living and is rarely seen. A number of Black File Snakes have been captured by scientists recently, and all of these were caught in traps at night. Otherwise they have been found in deserted termite mounds and under plant debris. This snake feeds on lizards and frogs. Females lay up to 6 eggs. When cornered, the Black File Snake may move in jerky movements while hiding its head under body coils. It also excretes a foul-smelling substance from glands in the tail region when handled.

▲
The Black File Snake is much smaller than the Southern File Snake, averaging 450 mm in length.

File snakes are quite common in some areas, but they are very secretive and are seldom seen.
▼

▲
When threatened, the Black File Snake moves in jerky movements and will hide its head under its coils.

Tell-tale signs

- Broad, flat head, distinct from the rest of the body
- Body is triangular with rough scales
- Active at night and rarely seen
- May be seen on tarred roads at night after warm summer rains

Egg-eaters

▲
A Common
Egg-eater.

Warren Schmidt

▲
All of the egg-eaters feed exclusively on birds' eggs.

There are 3 species of egg-eater in southern Africa. They are uniquely African snakes that are specially adapted for feeding on bird's eggs, which they appear to be able to locate from great distances. Once the egg is found it is swallowed whole, even if it is three or four times the size of the snake's head. Bony projections in the neck region are used to crack the egg. The shell is crushed, the contents of the egg swallowed, and the shell regurgitated as a neat package. This entire process can take as little as a few minutes, depending on the size of the egg. Egg-eaters have virtually no teeth and are completely harmless.

The **Common** or **Rhombic Egg-eater** averages 500 mm in length. It is light brown with dark and light blotches down the back, and dark V-markings on the neck, behind the head. The rounded head is slightly distinct from the rest of the body and the eyes are medium sized. The Common Egg-eater is widely distributed throughout most of southern Africa, except for true desert and closed-canopy forest. This nocturnal snake occurs in a variety of habitats and is frequently found in deserted termite mounds, and under rocks or loose bark. Females lay up to 25 eggs and may produce more than one clutch per season. When threatened, this snake will coil and uncoil in one

▲
Egg-eaters climb into trees and shrubs to search for eggs, which they probably locate using their sense of smell.

spot with the body inflated and the rough scales rubbing against one another, causing a hissing sound similar to that made by many adders. The snake will also gape, exposing the black mouth interior, like a Black Mamba, and will strike slowly but repeatedly, making sure it doesn't make contact and reveal that it doesn't have teeth.

The **Southern Brown Egg-eater** averages 700 mm in length and is plain yellowish red to reddish-brown in colour. This snake is found from the Eastern Cape northwards into KwaZulu-Natal, Swaziland and Mpumalanga. It inhabits grassland and open coastal woodland and hunts for birds' eggs at night. Females lay up to 17 eggs.

The **East African Egg-eater** averages around 500 mm in length. It differs from the Common Egg-eater in that it has a dark, broad band down the back, interrupted by white blotches. This snake occurs from lowland forest to moist savanna in northern Zululand, northwards into Mozambique and Eastern Zimbabwe. Females lay up to 28 eggs in summer.

▲
The Southern Brown Egg-eater lacks markings and is usually a reddish-brown to golden-brown colour.

The East African Egg-eater differs from the Common Egg-eater in appearance in that it has a dark band with white speckling down its body.
▼

The Common Egg-eater mimics venomous adders for self-defence. The body pattern is similar to that of some of the adders, including dark V-markings in the neck region. It coils and uncoils, rubbing its scales to emit a hissing sound, not unlike that made by some adders.

Tell-tale signs

- May have one or two dark V-markings on the neck behind the head and is uniform yellowish-red to reddish-brown with strongly-keeled scales
- May coil and uncoil in one spot, creating a hissing sound by rubbing its scales against one another
- Only active at night
- Often found in deserted termite mounds
- Always regurgitate crushed egg shells

Blind Snakes

Blind snakes are primitive snakes with cylindrical bodies and highly polished, tight-fitting scales. They have very small heads and the head and tail are not always distinguishable. The mouth is underslung and has no teeth on the lower jaw. As these are burrowing snakes that spend most of their lives underground and out of sight, their eyes are reduced and are often only visible as a dark spot beneath the skin. The tail ends in a sharp spike that is used to anchor them against a burrow while the head is forced forward like a bulldozer. These snakes feed largely on termites. All of the blind snakes are harmless.

▲
The Flowerpot Snake is a recent introduction to South Africa and is parthenogenetic: they are all females and do not need males to reproduce.

It is difficult to tell one end of Delalande's Beaked Blind Snake from the other.
▼

The **Flowerpot Snake** reaches an average length of about 150 mm. It is dark grey to brown in colour with a creamy snout. This is an introduced snake that is now well established in South Africa and is expanding its range rapidly. There are well-established populations in Durban and Cape Town. It is suspected that it was initially transported to the region in pot plants, hence the common

Warren Schmidt

Marius Burger

▲
Delalande's Beaked Blind Snake shows a distinct beak on the nose.

▲
Blind snakes all look very similar and have highly polished scales that give them a shiny appearance.

name. This species is an all-female or parthenogenetic snake – unfertilized ova develop within the female, allowing her to lay fertile eggs without having to mate. Up to 6 minute eggs are produced in summer, and measure a mere 40 mm upon hatching; one of the smallest snake hatchlings in the world.

Delalande's Beaked Blind Snake averages 250 mm in length, but can grow to 350 mm. It is a pale grey-brown snake with pale-edged scales, and has a chequered appearance. This is a widespread snake that occurs from the Western Cape, northwards into Namibia, Free State, Northern Cape, Gauteng, northern KwaZulu-Natal, Swaziland, Mpumalanga, North West, Limpopo, Zimbabwe and eastern Botswana. Individuals may be found in deserted termite mounds or on the surface after heavy summer rains. Females lay up to 8 eggs.

Schinz's Beaked Blind Snake averages 150–200 mm in length. It is pink above with dark blotches down the back. This snake is restricted to the drier west and occurs from the Karoo into Namaqualand, and into Namibia. It burrows into hard soil and is seldom encountered, except when it crosses roads at night.

Schlegel's Beaked Blind Snake reaches 1 m in length and has a varied coloration. It is usually dark brown to black above, or yellow-green to brownish-yellow with dark blotches. This is by far the largest blind snake in southern Africa. Adults may be extremely fat, especially towards the back, as they store fat to survive the long winter period. It occurs from Zululand, through Swaziland into Mpumalanga province and Mozambique. When handled, it has the habit of digging its sharply pointed tail into the hand. Between 8 and 60 eggs are laid, which hatch within 5–6 weeks.

Bibron's Blind Snake reaches an average legnth of around 350 mm. It is shiny dark brown to olive-brown in colour and is easily confused with other blind snakes. This snake may also be confused with the Southern Stiletto Snake. It occurs in the Eastern Cape, KwaZulu-Natal, Lesotho, Gauteng, North West, Limpopo and Zimbabwe. This is one of the more common Blind Snakes, and it inhabits coastal forest to moist savanna. Females lay up to 14 eggs.

▲
Schinz's Beaked Blind Snake has dark blotches down its body.

▲
Schlegel's Beaked Blind Snake is the largest of the blind snakes, reaching almost 1 m.

▲
Bibron's Blind Snake is found in the eastern half of South Africa and is the most commonly encountered of the blind snakes.

Tell-tale signs

- Difficult to distinguish head from the tail
- Eyes are minute and usually visible as a dark spot beneath the skin
- Some have beaked snouts
- Body is smooth, shiny and cylindrical

Worm or Thread Snakes

This snake looks like a small worm.

▼

These small, thin little snakes often resemble worms, and it is difficult to distinguish the head from the tail. They are burrowing snakes with cylindrical bodies and minute eyes that are barely visible under the skin as dark spots. Their diet consists of termites, ants and fleas, and they have no teeth in the upper jaw. All of these snakes are completely harmless.

▲
Peters' Worm Snakes are very small, thin snakes with highly polished scales.

Randy Babb

▲
Peters' Worm Snake feeds on termites, ants and fleas and is completely harmless.

The Cape Worm Snake is only found in the southern and Western Cape.

The **Long-tailed Worm Snake** has an average length of 150 mm and a maximum of 255 mm. It is grey above with a fleshy pink tinge. This snake occurs from Mpumalanga into Swaziland, Limpopo, Mozambique, eastern Botswana and Zimbabwe. As worm snakes spend most of their lives underground, they are seldom seen, unless exposed when rocks or logs are lifted. They are quick to disappear down the closest hole or to wriggle into sand if exposed. About 3 minute eggs are laid in summer.

The **Cape Worm Snake** averages 150 mm in length and, like several other worm snakes, is dark brown to black above. This snake is confined to the Western, southern and Eastern Cape. It spends most of its time underground in search of food. Large numbers of these snakes have been found congregating in suitable hiding places in winter.

Peters' Worm Snake is reddish-brown to black above and averages 200 mm in length, with a maximum length of 280 mm. This snake occurs from the Free State into Gauteng, North West, Limpopo, Mpumalanga, Mozambique, Zimbabwe, Botswana and Namibia. Individuals have been found in deserted termite mounds, under rocks and rotting logs, and also under cow dung. Females lay up to 7 elongate eggs that resemble rice grains. The eggs may be joined like little sausages.

The **Namaqua Worm Snake** has an average length of 200 mm with a maximum of 325 mm. It is light brown to purplish-brown above, with pale-edged scales that give it a chequered appearance. This snake is found in karoo scrub and in the Namib Desert from Namaqualand and the Richtersveld northwards into Namibia. Nothing is known of this snake's reproduction, but it is believed to be egg-laying.

Leonard Hoffman / IOA

It is very difficult to tell which end is the head and which is the tail of Peters' Worm Snake.

Long-tailed Worm Snakes have minute eyes that are barely visible under the skin.

Tell-tale signs

- Eyes are minute and concealed under the skin
- Body is cylindrical
- Difficult to differentiate the head from the tail
- Small and dark with highly polished scales that give a shiny appearance
- Seldom seen, unless excavated or flushed to the surface after heavy rains

Glossary

Amphisbaenid: Worm lizard – a legless, burrowing lizard.

Antivenom: Serum produced using the antibodies of horses that have been injected with venom. It combats the effect of snakebite by blocking access of toxic enzymes to target cells in a victim's body.

Aquatic: Living in water.

Arboreal: Living predominantly in trees.

Clutch: A hatch of eggs all laid at one time.

Cytotoxic: (of venom) Adversely affecting tissue and cell formation.

Diurnal: Being active mainly during the day.

Endemic: (of organisms) Found only in a specific area.

Fang: Specialized tooth adapted for the injection of venom.

Fossorial: Adapted to burrowing and living below ground.

Haemotoxic: (of venom) Compromising red blood cells or other components of the circulatory system, adversely affecting the blood or the functioning of the circulatory system.

Hatchling: A newborn snake produced by an egg-laying species.

Hemipenes: A pair of reproductive organs present in male snakes, lizards and amphisbaenids.

Incubation: Keeping eggs warm and humid to ensure continuous development.

Jacobson's organ: A pair of organs situated in the roof of the mouth, into which the tips of the forked tongue are pressed in order to taste and smell scent particles picked up by the tongue from its immediate environment.

Keeled: (of scales) Having a prominent ridge.

Necrosis: The death of cells in the body, usually within a localized area.

Neurotoxic: (of venom) Adversely affecting neuro-muscular function.

Oviparous: Egg-laying.

Parthenogenetic: Able to develop fertile eggs without mating.

Recurved: (of teeth) Bending backwards.

Rhombic: Having a diamond-shaped pattern.

Riverine: Pertaining to rivers.

Sidewind: Sideways movement of a section of the body, followed by the next section. Often seen in desert snakes on unstable dune sand, where usual forms of locomotion are not effective.

Viviparous: Giving birth to live offspring from eggs that hatch within the uterus or as the egg is laid, or shortly after laying.

Marius Burger

The Coral Shield Cobra blends with the colouring of its rocky habitat.

Index of names

Page references in *italics* indicate photographs.

A

adders 10-13, 15-20, 22-33, 64-65,
    84-85, 87
Adder
    Albany 29, *29*
    Berg 12, 22, 25, *25*
    Burrowing 54
    Common Night 32-33, *32*
    Desert Mountain 27, *27*
    Gaboon 10, *10*, 12, 17, 22, 24, *24*
    Horned 13, 26, *26*
    Many-horned 27, *27*, 28-29
    Namaqua Dwarf 13, *30*, 31, *95*
    Night 15, 33, 65
    Péringuey's 13, *18*, 31, *31*
    Plain Mountain 28, *28*
    Puff *5*, 10-11, 13, 15, 18-19, *19*, 20, *20*, 22,
        22, 23, *23*, 41, 84, 85
    Red 28, *28*
    Snouted Night 33, *33*
    Southern 12, 29, *29*
Asp, Burrowing 54

B

Bird Snake 52-53
Black Snake, Natal 55, *55*, 66
blind snakes 67, 88-89
Blind Snake
    Bibron's 89, *89*
    Delalande's Beaked *88*, 89
    Schinz's Beaked 89, *89*
    Schlegel's Beaked 89, *89*
Boomslang *3*, 14-16, 19, *19*, 48, *48*, 49, *49*, 50,
    50, 51, *51*, 52-53
bush snakes 14-15, 17, 35, 78-79
Bush Snake
    Spotted 78, *78*, 79
    Variegated 15

C

cobras 11-13, 15, 17, 19-21, 36-47,
    50, 52,
Cobra
    Anchieta's 38, *38*
    Black Spitting 41, *41*
    Black-necked Spitting 41, *41*
    Cape *6*, 13, 20, *20*, 21, 36, *36*, 37, 41, 77
    Egyptian 37
    Forest 12, *38*, 39, *39*
    Mozambique Spitting 20, *20*, 40, *40*,
        41, 43

Cobra continued
    Shield
        Coral *11*, 44, *44*, 45, *45*, *92*
        Eastern 47
        Kalahari 47, *47*
        Lowveld *46*, 47, *47*
        Namibian *44*, 45
    Snouted 20, 37, *37*, 38
    Zebra 42, *42*

E

egg-eaters 10, 13, 15-16, 86-87
Egg-eater
    Common 15, 86, *86*, 87
    East African 87, *87*
    Rhombic *8*, *10*, 13, 15, 86
    Southern Brown 87, *87*

F

file snakes 84-85
File Snake
    Black 85, *85*
    Southern 84, *84*, 85
Flowerpot Snake 88, *88*

G

grass snakes 12, 17, 21, 60
Grass Snake
    Grey-bellied *60*
    Olive *21*
green snakes 12, 50, 64, 78-79
Green Snake
    Angola 78
    Eastern Natal 79, *79*
    Western Natal 79, *79*

H

Herald Snake 19, 64, *64*, 65, *65*
house snakes 11, 13, 15-17, 19, 70-72
House Snake
    Aurora *1*, 72, *72*
    Brown 11, 13, 16-17, 19, 70, *70*, 71
    Fisk's 72
    Olive 71, *71*, 72
    Yellow-bellied

I

Ivuzamanzi 74

M

mambas 12, 14-15, 17, 19-21, 34-35, 50, 52, 84-85

Mamba
   Black 19-20, *20*, 21, 34, *34*, 35, 57, 87
   Green 12, 14, 34-35, *35*, 50, 79
M'fezi 40
Mole Snake 19, 33, 54, 76, *76*, 77, *77*

P

purple-glossed snakes 66-67
Purple-glossed Snake
   Common *66*, 67, *67*
   Natal 66, *66*
pythons 11, 14-16, 18-19, 68-69
Python
   Anchieta's Dwarf 69, *69*
   Royal 69
   Southern African 15-16, 18-19, 68, *68*, 69, *69*

R

Rattlesnake 68, 69
Red-lipped Snake 64, 65, *65*
Rinkhals 12, 15, 41, 43, *43*, 47, 61
rock snakes 70, 72-73
Rock Snake
   Spotted 13-15, 73, *73*
   Swazi *72*

S

sand snakes 13, 15, 17, 19, 56-61
Sand Snake
   Eastern Stripe-bellied *58*
   Jalla's *58*
   Western Stripe-bellied 56, *56*, *58*
Side-stabbing Snake 54
skaapstekers 18, 60-61
Skaapsteker
   Rhombic 18, 60
   Spotted 60, *60*, 61
   Striped 61, *61*
slug-eaters 80-81
Slug-eater
   Common 80, *80*, 81
   Variegated 81, *81*
stiletto snakes 54-55, 82-83, 89
Stiletto Snake
   Beaked *54*, 55
   Eastern Congo 55
   Southern 54, *54*, 82, 89

T

thread snakes 90-91
tiger snakes 13, 17, 19, 62-63
Tiger Snake
   Beetz's *9*, 63, *63*
   Common 62, *62*, 63

V

vine snakes 16, 19, 52-53
Vine Snake
   Eastern 53, *53*
   Oates' *52*, 53
   Southern *52*, 53, *53*
Viper
   Mole 54
   Pit 68, 69

W

water snakes 19, 74-75, 79
Water Snake
   Common Brown 19, 74, *74*, 75
   Dusky-bellied 75, *75*
   Green 79, *79*
whip snakes 56-59, 60-61
Whip Snake
   Cape *58*
   Crossed *57*, 59, *59*
   Dwarf 56, *59*
   Kalahari *58*
   Karoo *58*
   Leopard *59*
   Namib *59*
   Olive 56, *56*, 57
   Short-snouted *57*, 58, *58*
   Western *59*
wolf snakes 16, 82-83
Wolf Snake
   Common 82, *82*
   Pygmy 83, *83*
   Variegated 83, *83*
worm snakes 90-91
Worm Snake
   Cape 91, *91*
   Long-tailed 91, *91*
   Namaqua 91
   Peters' *90*, 91, *91*

A Namaqua Dwarf Adder from Port Nolloth.